0-8057-6646-4 $21.95

CLAUDE LÉVI-STRAUSS

Claude Lévi-Strauss and his works are at the forefront of the structuralist movement that has dominated literary theory and criticism since the 1960s. An acknowledged giant in the field of ethnology, Lévi-Strauss recorded the myths, rituals, and religious practices of primitive cultures and analyzed them as narrative stories according to a strict methodology that he codified in his ground-breaking studies *Race and History* and *Structural Anthropology and Totemism*. Lévi-Strauss's theories—involving binary logic, organic structure, the nature of myths, and the process of transformation—helped to establish the new science of structural anthropology, as well as other humanistic disciplines. Linguists and literary critics who adopted his imaginative terminology and methodology further developed the study of semiotics, or 'science of signs'. Applying rigorous logic to the interpretation of the literatures of a variety of cultures, Lévi-Strauss and his followers sought to discover within narrative forms the hidden structures and unconscious organizing principles that govern the creative process.

Roland A. Champagne approaches Lévi-Strauss's diverse writings by illuminating their unifying theme: the effort to define and understand the universal patterns of human thought and communication. Champagne examines Lévi-Strauss's methods as an anthropologist and as a writer-semiotician, and he demonstrates that Lévi-Strauss's seminal works contributed to the formulation of contemporary literary theory. With its effective rendition of Lévi-Strauss's complex theories of language as communication, as narrative, and as a sign of cultural identity,

Claude Lévi-Strauss

Twayne's World Authors Series
French Literature

David O'Connell, Editor

University of Illinois at Chicago

TWAS 792

CLAUDE LÉVI-STRAUSS
(1908-   )
Photograph courtesy of Suhrkamp Verlag.

Claude Lévi-Strauss

By Roland A. Champagne

University of Missouri–St. Louis

Twayne Publishers
A Division of G. K. Hall & Co. • *Boston.*

Claude Lévi-Strauss

Roland A. Champagne

Copyright © 1987 by G. K. Hall & Co.
All Rights Reserved
Published by Twayne Publishers
A Division of G. K. Hall & Co.
70 Lincoln Street
Boston, Massachusetts 02111

Copyediting supervised by Lewis DeSimone
Book production by Kristina Hals
Book design by Barbara Anderson

Typeset in 11 pt. Garamond
by Modern Graphics, Inc., Weymouth, Massachusetts

Printed on permanent/durable acid-free paper
and bound in the United States of America

Library of Congress Cataloging-in-Publication Data

Champagne, Roland A.
    Claude Lévi-Strauss.

    (Twayne's world authors series ; TWAS 792. French literature)
    Bibliography: p.
    Includes index.
    1. Lévi-Strauss, Claude.   2. Semiotics.   3. Structural
anthropology.   I. Title.   II. Series: Twayne's world authors series ; TWAS 792.
III. Series: Twayne's world authors series. French literature.
GN21.L4C48   1987   302.2′092′4 [B]   87–17695
ISBN 0–8057–6646–4 (alk. paper)

Ani l'dodi v'dodi li.

Contents

About the Author

Roland Champagne is professor of French and associate dean of the College of Arts & Sciences at the University of Missouri-St. Louis. His master's thesis (1972) and doctoral dissertation (1974) were on the work of Philippe Sollers. He is the author of *Beyond the Structuralist Myth of Ecriture* (1977) and *Literary History in the Wake of Roland Barthes* (1984). His interests in aesthetics, literary theory, and creative fiction have led to essays on contemporary French writers such as Maurice Blanchot, Jacques Derrida, Marguerite Duras, Michel Serres, and Julia Kristeva for journals such as *Sub-stance,* the *French Review, New Literary History,* and *Centrum.*

Preface

Claude Lévi-Strauss is a prolific writer whose ethnological studies had become identified as "structuralist" by the mid-1960s. His intentions were somewhat at odds with how others understood his complicated schematics and detailed analyses. Nevertheless, throughout his career Lévi-Strauss has been concerned with how human beings communicate with one another, both with and without the use of words.

Whereas some of his critics have accused him of being antihumanistic, this study will focus upon his contributions to the humanistic concerns of semiotics, that study defined by A. J. Greimas as showing how men and women conceive of the world and organize while also humanizing it. [1] Lévi-Strauss openly admits that his analyses of myths and rites involve understanding them as modes of communication. However, he also insists upon his identity as a scientist analyzing peoples without a heritage in writing and thereby discovering systems of human thought. Despite his conscious designs for analysis, he is a humanist who today demonstrates to us the catharsis of his writing. As an ethnographer, a writer of ethnology, he recorded and narrated stories of the human spirit as he recast myths, rituals, and religions into structures and systems.

My presentation will take the deliberate bias of Lévi-Strauss the writer-semiotician. A caveat must be acknowledged in that this "writer-semiotician" also assumed many other identities—as scientist, philosopher, historian, anthropologist, traveler, translator, sociologist, psychologist, literary critic, intellectual, among others, deliberate or not. As semiotician-writer, he can be understood in all these guises without the need either to prioritize or to preclude any others.

His contributions to semiotics will be discussed as separate items in each chapter. After the initial chapter giving a general background to his life and synopses of his writings, there will be nine chapters each presenting specific components of the views of communication perpetuated by Lévi-Strauss the writer.

His positions regarding binary logic, organic structure, the nature of myth, and the role of transformation will be discussed initially.

These are the primary components in the intellectual patterns he identified in the human spirit. These constituent elements lead me in the sixth and subsequent chapters to consider his methods, both as an anthropologist and as an intellectual. These methods entail the adoption of a humanistic role: to help us understand what distinguishes human communication. I return to the "humanizing" function of semiotics, as previously cited from Greimas, because Lévi-Strauss pertinently demonstrated how men and women conceive of and organize the world. The concomitant activity of humanizing the world while forming it and shaping it intellectually was elaborated by the French ethnologist in his cross-cultural opus. With these parameters for my discussion, I will examine his methods, working to reveal the opposition of nature and culture, the role of history, the symbolic order, and the importance of nonconscious thinking as constituent elements in the "new humanism," a vision resulting from the communications of Lévi-Strauss. Despite criticism from some of his contemporaries, he did realize what Luc de Heusch described as his main ambition: to contribute to the "science of signs" at the heart of social life.[2] Thus, Claude Lévi-Strauss has become a humanistic semiotician for our times and for all time.

I have benefited during the preparation of this volume from David O'Connell for his act of faith, from Anne Butler for her words, from Judy Camigliano for her patience and organization, from Peter Wolfe for pertinent articles, from Brian Vandenberg for inspiring dialogues, from Gert for Sunday afternoons, and from Nina for honesty.

Roland A. Champagne

University of Missouri–St. Louis

Chronology

1908   Claude Lévi-Strauss born to the artist Raymond Lévi-Strauss and Emma Lévy on Saturday, 28 November, in Brussels, Belgium.

1914   Raymond Lévi-Strauss moves family to Versailles, France, to live with his father, a middle-class rabbi.

1927   Claude studies philosophy at the Sorbonne until 1931; classmates include Simone de Beauvoir and Maurice Merleau-Ponty.

1931   *Agrégé* in philosophy and law with honors from Sorbonne.

1932   Marries Dina Dreyfus; teaches in a lycée in Mont-de-Marsan, France, until 1934.

1934   Célestin Bouglès, Director, Ecole Normale Supérieure, recommends Claude as professor of sociology at University of São Paolo, Brazil, until 1937; Claude reads Robert Lowie's *Primitive Society* (1920) and decides to become an ethnologist.

1936   First anthropological publication, a forty-five page article on the social organization of the Bororo Indians of Brazil.

1938   Participates in Franco-Brazilian expedition to the interior of Brazil (Mato Grosso; Amazonas) until 1939; Marcel Mauss invents "social anthropology."

1940   Returns to France and becomes liaison officer on Maginot Line for the mobilized French Army.

1941   Aunt Aline Caro-Delvaille, in New York City since World War I, helps him to emigrate to the United States; faculty member at New School for Social Research until 1945; Rockefeller Foundation support; meets Roman Jakobson.

1944   Teaches at Barnard College.

1946   Cultural attaché to French Embassy in Washington until 1947; marries Rose Marie Ullmo after divorcing Dreyfus; later has son Laurent with Rose Marie.

1947   Co-founds with Emile Benveniste, Pierre Gourou, and André

Leroi-Gourhon and then edits *L'Homme,* French review of anthropology.

1948   Receives Doctorat ès Lettres from University of Paris; adjunct director of the Musée de l'Homme, Paris; publishes *La Vie familiale et sociale des Indiens Nambikwara.*

1949   *Les Structures elémentaires de la parenté.*

1950   Director of Studies (Social Anthropology Laboratory) at École Pratique des Hautes Études; publishes introduction to the work of Marcel Mauss; field trip to Chittagong, East Pakistan.

1952   *Race et histoire.*

1953   Secretary General, International Council of Social Sciences until 1960.

· 1954   Marries Monique Roman after divorcing Ullmo; later has son Matthieu with Monique.

1955   *Tristes tropiques* and articles "Les Mathématiques de l'homme" and "The Anthropological Study of Myth."

1958   *Anthropologie structurale.*

1960   Chair of Social Anthropology, Collège de France; publishes "Le Geste d'Asdiwal"; Jean-Paul Sartre publishes critique of his ethnological method; publishes "Structure et forme," distinguishing between "structure" and Vladimir Propp's "form."

1961   English translation of *Tristes tropiques* as *A World on the Wane* by John Russell appears; publishes with Jakobson structuralist model for literary criticism, a reading of "Les Chats."

1962   *Le Totemisme aujourd'hui* and volume 2 of *L'Anthropologie structurale;* honorary doctorate, University of Brussels.

1963   Debate with Paul Ricoeur; publishes *La Pensée sauvage;* signs "Manifeste des 121" against the Algerian War; translations *Structural Anthropology* and *Totemism* appear.

1964   Honorary doctorate, Oxford University; publishes volume 1 of *Mythologiques.*

1965   Honorary doctorate, Yale University.

1966   Volume 2 of *Mythologiques.*

1967   Honorary doctorate, University of Chicago.

1968   Volume 3 of *Mythologiques;* receives Gold Medal from the Centre National de la Recherche Scientifique.

1970   Honorary doctorate, Columbia University.

1971   Volume 4 of *Mythologiques.*

1972   Honorary doctorate, Stirling University.

1973   Elected to the Académie française.

1980   Most cited enthnologist in the world *(Le Nouvel Observateur).*

1981   France's most influential intellectual *(Lire).*

1982   Retires from Collège de France.

1983   *Le Regard éloigné.*

1985   *La Potière jalouse.*

1986   Honorary doctorate, Harvard University.

Chapter One
Lévi-Strauss despite Himself

Belgian Beginnings (1908–26)

From his birth Claude Lévi-Strauss inherited a creative thrust to express his own alterity. On Saturday, 28 November 1908, the artist Raymond Lévi-Strauss waited while his wife Emma Lévy gave birth to their son Claude in Brussels. Six years later, Raymond's aesthetic interests became incompatible with the intrusions of the Great War. He had come to Belgium to do a series of portraits, but the Belgian countryside was no longer idyllic, nor was Brussels a safe place to raise a family. It was a time when the social fabric of Belgium was being seriously questioned. The socialist Henri De Man was beginning to have intellectual influence upon the developing fascist ideology that was to take hold of Europe after the war. It certainly was no place for an artist who depended upon the bourgeoisie to buy his work in order to care for his family. So Raymond Lévi-Strauss took his wife and the young Claude to France, where, in Versailles, they could find refuge with and some financial assistance from Raymond's father, a middle-class rabbi. That move in 1914 brought the young Claude into a Jewish and French environment that was not his by birth. An outsider to both traditions, he did not easily assimilate either one.

Claude's artistic heritage, passed on from his father and two uncles—all artists—did give him the creative impulse to express his otherness through the field of ethnology. This area of interest was an adopted field, not his own by education or training. He received no formal academic preparation, in Belgium or in France, for ethnology. The French use the word *ethnology* in the sense that Americans have for *anthropology*. In France, ethnology was not yet a distinct discipline worthy of study at the university. Claude Lévi-Strauss adopted the avocation of ethnology after having studied it in the writings of the Americans Robert Lowie, Franz Boas, and A. L. Kroeber. He adapted what he read and created his own identity

1

as ethnologist such that he would eventually be heralded as the founder of "structuralist anthropology."

And so the young Claude inherited Belgian, Jewish, and later, American beginnings that differentiated him from his French neighbors. Even during his later professional years as a writing anthropologist, he noted that his translated works often failed to reflect his thought processes. Although he was specifically referring to the problems of translating his French writings into English, his complaint is indicative of his situation of otherness, of not being translatable, and of his search for the natural language of communication.

Translated by Other Cultures (1927–39)

He received his education in philosophy and law at the Sorbonne in Paris from 1927 to 1932, when he became agrégé with honors in philosophy. Fellow students included Maurice Merleau-Ponty and Simone de Beauvoir, who would later review his *Les Structures elémentaires de la parenté* (1949; rev. 1967; translated as *Elementary Structures of Kinship,* 1969). In his *Tristes tropiques* (1955; translated as *A World on the Wane,* 1961; and *Tristes Tropiques,* 1981), he would have us understand his time at the Sorbonne as one of questioning the theoretical world of the philosophers and of espousing instead geology, Marxism, and psychoanalysis as his true handmaidens.

Nevertheless, Lévi-Strauss employed much of his writings to philosophize about the importance of ethnology or anthropology. He has indeed scorned this identity by insisting that he did not want to create a philosophy of structuralism.[1] But the outsider in him wanted to be accepted by the insiders. And the irony of this thinker is that he so succeeded in this unconscious need to be on the inside that his positions eventually came to be perceived as esoteric and even elitist among intellectuals worldwide. From his earliest writings, he wore the philosophical trappings of a twentieth-century Jean-Jacques Rousseau concerned, in an almost paranoiac fashion, with how "progress" had so infected the mores of society as to make us "prisoners of our own subjectivity."[2]

After his first marriage to Dina Dreyfus in 1932 and a two-year stint as a teacher in a lycée, Lévi-Strauss received the opportunity from Celestin Bouglès, the Director of the École Normale Supérieure in Paris, to travel to the University of São Paulo, Brazil, where he would become a professor of sociology. Since the University had been organized by French intervention, the French were still responsible for providing it with faculty personnel.

It was during 1934, when he was so enthralled by his experiences in Brazil and by his reading of Lowie's *Primitive Society* in English, that he decided to become an ethnologist. This stage of his life is parallel to that of the founder of the *Annales* school of history, Fernand Braudel, in that both of them were significantly affected by their experiences in Brazil early in their professional careers such that the whole orientation of their thinking took decisive turns. Braudel, after three months at the University of São Paulo in 1935, began to realize the impact that geography had on history (see, for example, his interview in *Magazine littéraire,* November 1984). Likewise, Lévi-Strauss was at the University of São Paulo from 1934 to 1937 when he formulated his key ideas about the opposition "inside-outside" and began to develop his theories about the relationships between cultural assimilation and difference. Perhaps it was there, too, that he shaped the "poetic" sensibility so obvious to the readers of *Tristes tropiques* and to some of his critics such as Edmund Leach, who remarked—however ironically—that "the philosopher-advocate is also a poet."[3]

By 1936, Claude Lévi-Strauss had already published his first piece, an article on the social organization of the Bororo Indians of Brazil. His stay in Brazil until 1939 gave him the opportunity to do the fieldwork which laid the foundation for many articles as well as his books *La Vie familiale et sociale des Indiens Nambikwara* (1948) and *Tristes tropiques.* Critics have disputed the quality of this research (he did not converse with the informants in their native languages) and the quantity (a five-month expedition to the interior of Brazil in 1938 and part of a Franco-Brazilian expedition to the Mato Grosso and the Amazonas in 1939) of his fieldwork. Nevertheless, the creative and prolific character of the work generated by these experiences cannot be denied.

Linguistics in the United States (1941–47)

Lévi-Strauss returned to France in time for his mobilization in the "phoney war," during which he served as a liaison officer until the Occupation. Once again the outsider as a Jew in a hostile environment, he emigrated, with the help of his aunt who had been living in New York City since World War I, by way of Puerto Rico and Martinique to the United States in 1941. There he began his association with the New School for Social Research in New York City under sponsorship by the Rockefeller Foundation. There, too, he began his lifelong association with the Prague School linguist Roman Jakobson. The Prague School of linguistics had done phonological analyses during the 1930s which later provided the bases for founding "structural linguistics" as a distinct endeavor. Within the environment of the developing field of structural linguistics, Lévi-Strauss published an article on the ties between structural analysis in linguistics and anthropology in a 1945 issue of *Word*, the official journal of the Jakobson group at the New School. Jakobson's influence led to many linguistically oriented publications for Lévi-Strauss, especially as the coauthor of a study analyzing Baudelaire's "Les Chats" (*L'Homme* 2 [1962]). This analysis, purporting to be an example of "structuralist" literary criticism, engendered an extended controversy with Michael Riffaterre about the limitations of the method's application in appreciating poetry. Nevertheless, Lévi-Strauss continued his training in structural linguistics until 1947. During this period he taught at Barnard College and became editor of *L'Homme*, the French journal of anthropology.

The article published in *Word* in 1945 ("L'Analyse structurale en linguistique et en anthropologie") set the tone for much of his later writings. It would become his hallmark to apply the structural method of linguistics to ethnological material heretofore considered as disparate data by linguists. Lévi-Strauss set out to demarcate a specific arena for ethnology in which he would be the insider. Here again, he realized a marriage of differences to speak to us about how we communicate. Rather than working within single systems, he combined various humanized objects whose nature had been vitiated by the isolated approaches of the sciences. He sought to break down the barriers between linguistics and the social sciences, for example, by speaking of the "ideology of copper"[4] among tribes considered to be outside of "civilization" proper. We must, however, point out a caveat in this apparent case of cultural assimilation. Jacques Derrida has correctly reprehended his "phonologism"[5] (i.e., the single logic or mode of thinking) of modeling work upon the single discipline of linguistics, and even more singularly, the specific model of structural linguistics. Nevertheless, the work of Lévi-Strauss has survived this limitation by demonstrating the subtle communication of peoples who reveal their humanity through storytelling in languages that are not always obvious ones.

During 1946–47, Claude Lévi-Strauss was the cultural attaché to the French Embassy in New York City. In that capacity, he hosted the increasingly popular Albert Camus, who first came to New York on 25 March 1946 and was detained because of his Communist party membership. Lévi-Strauss did not personally come to the aid of Camus on that occasion, according to Herbert Lottman.[6] Some might say that Claude Lévi-Strauss did not want to become politically enmeshed in the affair. During Camus's three-month visit, Lévi-Strauss did not have much to do with him. But he did introduce Camus to Chinatown and to the cabarets of the Bowery, much to Camus's appreciation because that is the part of New York that Camus enjoyed the best.[7]

It was a hectic time with some bittersweet moments for Lévi-Strauss. He was divorced from Dina Dreyfus and in 1946 married Rose Marie Ullmo, who later bore him the son Laurent.

Structural Anthropologist (1948–60)

During 1948–49, Lévi-Strauss returned to Paris as the adjunct director of the Musée de l'Homme. While there, he earned his degree Doctorat ès Lettres and saw the publication of his *La Vie familiale et sociale des Indiens Nambikwara* (1948) and *Les Structures élémentaires de la parenté*. No mere taxonomy, this second book adapted Marcel Mauss's theory of gifts to kinship and revealed kinship to be a nonconscious structure by which women become media of exchange between social groups. He received the Prix Paul Pelliot for this book and soon gained the attention of feminists from Simone de Beauvoir (a former classmate) to the present-day Jane Gallop (see her *The Daughter's Seduction,* 1978) for the attention he thus brought to a pervasive cross-cultural problem.

After a field trip to Chittagong, East Pakistan, in 1950, he received an appointment in the École des Hautes Études and published an introduction to Marcel Mauss's collected works that appeared that same year. Lévi-Strauss was beginning to make a name for himself in his adopted homeland. From his post in Paris, he adopted a bold public position against colonization and racial prejudice in the UNESCO publication *Race et histoire* (1952; trans. *Race and History,* 1958). Thanks to this work and to an essay on the panoramic development of ethnology appearing in the journal *Diogène,* he became secretary-general of the International Council of Social Sciences, a position he would keep until 1960. His star was rising in 1954 as he married Monique Roman, with whom he would have yet another son in the coming years.

It was *Tristes tropiques* that was making Lévi-Strauss truly popular because of its exotic flavor and Rousseauvian tones of a return to nature in 1955 when the Korean War, the atomic bomb, and Communist aggression menaced "civilization." He offered alternative pursuits with this diary of his trip to Brazil and essays appearing that year: "Les Mathématiques de l'homme" and "The Structural Study of Myth." It should be noted that he had been writing in both English and French since his experience in New York during World War II. His mark or identity as a "structural anthropologist" was made with the appearance of *Anthropologie structurale* (1958; trans. *Structural Anthropology,* 1963). In 1959, Claude Lévi-Strauss earned an appointment at the Collège de France, where Mauss himself had invented the discipline of "social anthropology," thus finally arriving at the inside of a culture not his own.

Controversial Intellectual (1961–86)

His popularity was a two-edged sword. On the one hand, he became the incarnation of "structuralism" for many journals and newspapers concerned with the elitism of the latest intellectual fads in Paris. On the other hand, intellectuals throughout the world began to examine his work closely and to take him to task for the attention his work received. For example, his popularized coinage of *bricolage* ("handiwork" in the sense of tinkering) as the work of the ethnologist was called into question by Derrida, who wondered whether Lévi-Strauss really understood himself as the "handyman" or rather as an "engineer" who used his ingenuity and scientific training to construct models of communication.

Meanwhile, in 1960, Lévi-Strauss published the essay "Structure et forme" attempting to distinguish formalism from structuralism. Jean-Paul Sartre began a long-lasting debate with his former colleague at the Sorbonne, who had become renowned as "Sartre's admirer and friend."[8] The "analytical method" apparently adopted by Lévi-Strauss the scientist was refuted by Sartre in favor of the "dialectical method" with its involvement of observer, observed, and results. The arguments published in the journal *Critique* generated a certain defensiveness in Lévi-Strauss. He responded to Sartre in *La Pensée sauvage* (1961; trans. *The Savage Mind,* 1966), thus initiating a series of intellectual debates about the social "relevance" of "structuralism." Paul Ricoeur, the "hermeneutic" thinker, disputed what was called "the Kantian unconscious"[9] in that the mathematical organization of the structuralist method imposes systems on human thinking without acknowledging the role of consciousness. Lévi-Strauss, concerned about these critiques by major intellectuals, published interviews in order to regain control of how others perceived him and his contributions and to remain on the inside rather than on the outside of the French intelligentsia. Georges Charbonnier edited one book-length interview in 1961, the year in which John Russell also published the English-language translation of *Tristes tropiques.*

Controversy continued to follow Lévi-Strauss as he published with Roman Jakobson an analysis of Charles Baudelaire's sonnet "Les Chats." The article purported to be an exemplary application of structural linguistics to literature. Michael Riffaterre of Columbia University, however, took exception to the changes wrought upon a poem by the imposition of scientific rules of observation.

Despite (or perhaps because of) the controversies, Lévi-Strauss published a collection of essays (*Anthropologie structurale,* 2) and a study of totemism (*Le Totemisme aujourd'hui,* 1962; trans. *Totemism,* 1962). In 1962, he received an honorary doctorate from the Université Libre of Brussels. His native country had finally recognized him. He was now an insider looking out. Indeed, he began to stimulate a fashionable concern with "structuralism" by creating envy in those on the "outside" of his coterie. After joining other French intellectuals in signing the "Manifeste des 121" against the Algerian War, he received an honorary doctorate from Oxford University and began his four-volume series about the myths of Indian cultures in North America (*Mythologiques*). As his work became more and more available through translations worldwide, he asserted his defiance to those who resented his esoteric and modish audience: "you can also wonder if this so-called structuralism is not around only to serve as an alibi for the untenable boredom emanating from contemporary literature."[10]

Lévi-Strauss continued to receive accolades from renowned uni-

versities during the 1960s and the 1970s. He accepted honorary
degrees from Yale (1965), Chicago (1967), Columbia (1970), Stirling (1972), and Harvard (1986). He was admitted to the ultimate
inner sanctum by being elected to the Académie française in 1973.
Popularity soon followed as he was voted France's most influential
intellectual by the readers of the journal *Lire* in April 1981 and was
identified as the most cited ethnologist in the world between 1969
and 1977 (*Le Nouvel observateur,* 28 June 1980). Thus, he has achieved
the recognition, both intellectual and popular, of an insider.

And yet many of Lévi-Strauss's British colleagues are skeptical of
his popular recognition on the Continent and in the United States.
The anthropologist Edmund Leach exemplified this skepticism as
the gadfly to the "structuralist" type of anthropological research:
"British anthropologists . . . are alarmed by those strands in the
Lévi-Strauss brand of structuralism which seems to reduce all men
to a single pattern."[11] That alarm stemmed from what Leach called
"a confidence trick"[12] by Lévi-Strauss, who "often manages to give
me ideas even when I don't really know what he is saying."[13] The
mathematical formulas and the complicated schematics in the Lévi-
Strauss studies have dazzled and even mesmerized the best of his
colleagues.

And yet he is heuristic for his tenacity in analyzing what is "other"
and in creating models of how differentiation can tell us more about
how all of us think and share the common ground of humanity in
narration. Aware that his abstract diagrams intimidated some of his
readers, Lévi-Strauss told us in the fourth volume of his *Mythologiques*
(*L'Homme nu,* trans. *The Naked Man,* 1981) that "these tables are
illustrations, not to be used as proof, but especially didactically."[14]
His teachings were about the common "human spirit" that links
all humanity, no matter how different in race, nationality, or religion. I will examine the components of this spirit because his work
has expanded rather than evolved over the years so that even his
works *L'Identité* (1977), *Le Regard éloigné* (1983, trans. *The View from
Afar,* 1985) and *La Potière jalouse* (1985) are expansions of ideas he
promulgated during earlier works prior to the intellectual debates
in the later part of his career. Even these debates are crucial parts
of the teachings of Lévi-Strauss in that through them he brought
attention to his lifelong crusade: to help us understand that human
difference is only superficial and that we all seek to think and to
communicate in similar ways.

Within the Folds of His Books

Claude Lévi-Strauss published many essays individually and then reorganized them into collections published as books. For the convenience of potential readers who cannot know from the titles of his books which essays are contained therein, I will devote the next five sections of this chapter to outlining the contents of his books as well as the tenor of his major articles. These five sections correspond to the five major interests of his ethnographical or writing career: 1) his ethnological ambitions (The Aspiring Ethnologist); 2) the influence of structural linguistics (A Linguistic Ambience); 3) the analyses of cultural practices (Cultural Practices); 4) his search for the human spirit (Myths and More Myths); and 5) his theories about structuralism (On the Inside Looking Out). In these sections, I will offer synopses of the contents of his works because the contents are usually not obvious from the titles, especially since most of his books are anthologies of heterogeneous essays. In subsequent chapters of my presentation, I will elaborate upon the significance of what Lévi-Strauss said.

The Aspiring Ethnologist

1. "Contribution à l'étude de l'organisation sociale des Indiens Bororo." His first published article appeared in 1936 in the *Journal de la société des américanistes de paris* as a recollection from his visits in January and February of that year to the interior of Brazil. This article is one of his few analyses based on actual field visits to collect data himself. His presentation is limited to a geographical explanation of Bororo society. The physical layout of the hutches in concentric circles provides a model for the organization of the clans within the tribe. Some details are also given about cultural customs, such as the matrilineal kinship system, with sketches of the decorations of arrows, spears, and penis sheaths. There were already over twenty studies of the Bororo tribe when this article appeared. This study is distinguished by its link between the geography of the village and the social organization of the tribe.

2. *La Vie familiale et sociale des Indiens Nambikwara* (1948). Lévi-Strauss also used his expedition to the interior of the Amazon in Brazil, specifically to a plateau called the Mato Grosso, as a basis for his first book, a monograph about the Nambikwara Indians.

His presentation is divided into two main concerns: their family life and their social life.

The tribe was discovered by Western civilization in 1907. Its neighboring tribes, the Tupi and the Ge, are important because Lévi-Strauss considers the geographical milieu to be significant in comparing and contrasting the Nambikwara with or to their neighbors. Lévi-Strauss does attempt to give phonological representations of their language and, through an informant, distinguishes between men's and women's use of language. This dualism is traced to a psychological polarization within the family and the society of the Nambikwara. The society has a winter and a summer season. These dual seasons entail family life based in the winter on a sedentary, agricultural life in which men are the doers; in the summer, however, the Nambikwara pursue a nomadic, adventurous life whereby women provide family subsistence by harvesting and scavenging whatever they can. The first lifestyle is evoked by the Nambikwara with melancholy and acceptance of the human condition. The second lifestyle is characterized by them with excitement and a sense of discovery. Both of these poles in the Nambikwara familial and social structure have ramifications on their social, psychological, economic, and cultural makeup.

3. *Tristes tropiques* (1955).   In this memoir of his travel to Brazil during the 1930s, Lévi-Strauss provides an autobiographical presentation of the various people involved in his choice to go to São Paulo and his subsequent decision to become an ethnologist. The poetic, naturalistic style of the narrative appealed to many readers outside the related fields of anthropology.

The original edition had nine chapters: 1) "La Fin des voyages" ("Journeys' End"); 2) "Feuilles de route" ("Notes along the Way"); 3) "Le Nouveau Monde" ("The New World"); 4) "La Terre et les hommes" ("The Earth and Humanity"); 5) "Caduveo" ("The Caduveo Tribe"); 6) "Bororo" ("The Bororo Tribe"); 7) "Nambikwara" ("The Nambikwara Tribe"); 8) "Tupi-Kawahib" ("The Tupi-Kawahib Tribe"); and 9) "Le Retour" ("Coming Home"). Although the narrator claimed not to like travel logs, he set about writing one full of adventure and exoticism, in a style recalling Jean-Jacques Rousseau's reflections on the "state of nature" prior to the social organization of humanity, a cynical view of human progress, and an impressionistic view of the interaction of society and individuals.

Lévi-Strauss the narrator does deliberately refer to Rousseau as his predecessor. This work, however, is not simply a self-defense as was the *Confessions* of the eighteenth-century musician-philosopher. Instead, the narrator realizes more than Rousseau did that humanity means belonging to and interacting with social, cultural, geographical, and political factors.

The three tribes of the Mato Grosso in Brazil are explained here to exemplify a search for human origins across the repetitive patterns of human history. This is a nontechnical travel log with pictures of the natives and their artifacts. The narrator uses very little professional jargon or scholarship. The presentation appeals to a general audience, almost as a vehicle for the propagandizing of ethnological studies.

4. *Leçon inaugurale* (1970). Delivered as his acceptance speech at the Collège de France in 1960 when he assumed the chair in social anthropology, this address is appropriately entitled by the official translation into English as *The Scope of Anthropology*. He begins the address by noting the coincidence of structural and historical properties in myths. This coincidence is a model for the two faces of social anthropology, its present condition and its past.

The past is explained by recalling the research of Franz Boas (Anglo-American traditions), Marcel Mauss (his study of gifts), Emile Durkheim (sociological method), Malinowski (ethnology), and Radcliffe-Brown (comparative method). The present status of social anthropology is characterized by the uniqueness of its certain method, both empirical and deductive, in arriving at an inventory of societies and creating a system for categorizing even the most isolated primitive tribe. Ethnology is to be distinguished from anthropology because the former is concerned with reviving the past of a primitive people and, because of its precarious methods, offers very little to social anthropology. History and social anthropology can be helpful to one another. But Lévi-Strauss distinguishes between "cold" (limited human work force and mechanical functioning mark the zero of historical temperature) and "hot" (caste and class differentiations maximize a heated, productive era) to explain the special role of history for primitive peoples as opposed to the peoples of Western civilization. Above all, social anthropology must concern itself with those semiological artifacts and practices not addressed by linguistics, that is, with myths, rituals, kinship and marriage customs, and other cultural forms of economic exchange. He calls for a Renaissance whereby humanism can become the measure of humanity.

A Linguistic Ambience

1. *Anthropologie structurale* (1958; rev. 1974). Although the influence of linguistics upon the work of Lévi-Strauss dates to the 1940s when he was living in New York City, *Anthropologie structurale* provides some of his previously published articles dealing with the influence of linguistics on his ethnological studies. I point out specifically the following essays:

a) "L'analyse structurale en linguistique et en anthropologie" (reprinted from *Word*, Journal of the Linguistic Circle of New York, 1945): Since linguistics is a social science, it is appropriate for anthropologists to note its recent progress, especially in light of its methodological discoveries and its scientific pretensions. The phonological investigations by Troubetskoy reveal that historical explanations are inadequate to explain structural similarities in different systems. Superficial applications of phonological studies would be inadequate in ethnology. Nevertheless, the notions of "system" and "structure" are homologous between linguistic phonemes and the atomic components of kinship systems. Lévi-Strauss then posits the avuncular relationship as a key to kinship studies, "a kinship atom," which will help to reveal more complex structures and systems. Linguistics and anthropology can together help to explain the nature of symbolic thought.

b) "Linguistique et anthropologie" (translated from the original in English delivered to a conference in 1952): Discussion of the "human spirit" as a crucial bond between these two disciplines because of the interrelationship between language and culture.

c) "La notion de structure en ethnologie" (translated from the original in English published in *Anthropology Today*, 1953): The "structuralist" enterprise enables us to call into question the use of the term *structure* in ethnology. He reviews how history, sociology, ethnology, and ethnography have used *structure* as an inductive concept. Finally, he challenges modern ethnology with making *structure* an empirically driven, dynamic, and non-Formalist tool.

2. *Les structures élémentaires de la parenté* (1949; rep. 1967). This monograph was written in the United States between 1944

and 1947. It is based on relatively thin ethnological research on kinship. After World War II, societies such as those in the New Guinea Jungle became a rich source for ethnological investigation into kinship. Although Lévi-Strauss did not have access to these more recent works, his study of kinship provides a specific application of structural linguistic methods to an anthropological problem: the incest taboo.

Beginning with chapters on the passage from the state of nature to the state of culture and on prior theories about the incest taboo, he divides his presentation into restricted and open kinship systems. Both systems are marked by the incest taboo and the sophisticated exchange and gift-giving practices noted by Marcel Mauss. The linguistic notion of "structure" is applied to the marriage of cross cousins ("cousins croisés"), considered to be a basic atom of exchange in the societies surveyed. In all kinship systems, the passage to the state of culture is significant because of the economic dimension accompanying that state. Subsequently, material goods, symbols, and women became gifts exchanged within these societies. Thus, the exchange of women was the basis for marriage and the incest taboo in kinship systems. Edmund Leach, a contemporary anthropologist, disputes these conclusions by charging that Lévi-Strauss is so intent upon applying "structure" to kinship systems that he "disregards the empirical facts"[15] by confusing descent, the legal transmission of goods from one generation to another, with filiation, the biological link between parent and child.

3. "Charles Baudelaire's 'Les Chats.' " The linguistic model for structure became especially controversial subsequent to the appearance of this article coauthored with Roman Jakobson in 1962 in the French ethnological journal *L'Homme.* From the beginning of their analysis, the rhyme scheme of the sonnet is compared or contrasted with the grammar of the words. This tension sets the tone of the article for finding binary components, antinomies, dichotomies, etc. The reading is clearly based on revealing the dualisms within the poem. A theoretical system lurks behind the analysis. Jakobson's proposal that poetry is generated on the horizontal and vertical axes of metonymy and metaphor is substantiated on many levels by this reading which constantly refers to the oscillation and/or vacillation of the poet between polarities.

Cultural Practices

1. *Race et histoire* (1952; rep. 1967; rev. 1985). This UNESCO-commissioned pamphlet provided Claude Lévi-Strauss with the opportunity to rail against ethnocentrism and to situate the ethnologist within society. He also promotes an ethic of "dynamic tolerance" which I will discuss at length in chapter 10. In addition, he discusses the idea of "progress" as promoted by Western civilization to suggest a cleavage in the study of history between stationary and cumulative societies, whereby stationary refers to those whose "development" is not analogous to those who have accumulated achievements considered to be "progressive." Racism is the hegemonic result of societies with cumulative histories assimilating societies with stationary histories. The ethnologist must continue to demonstrate the need for tolerance in dominant civilizations to discourage racism.

2. *La Pensée sauvage* (1962). This work, whose title can be translated as either "the primitive mind" or "the savage mind" was published as a rebuttal to the "civilized mind." Generally, Lévi-Strauss argues that the mind of the so-called primitive is not naturally different from that of the "civilized" model. The "primitive" tends to be expressed through language and practices that are part of a daily routine of concrete reality.

The essay "La Science du concret" ("The Science of the Concrete") refers to the art of "bricolage" ("handiwork") by which representatives of all cultures select from heterogeneous repertoires in their environments components for myths and rituals peculiar to their societies.

Seven other essays in *La Pensée sauvage* are dedicated to demonstrating the integrity of the myths and rituals found among diverse isolated societies. These essays are: 1) "La Logique des classifications totémiques" ("The Logic of Totemic Classifications"); 2) "Les Systèmes de transformation" ("Systems of Transformations"); 3) "Totem et caste" ("Totem and Caste"); 4) "Catégories, éléments, espèces, nombres" ("Categories, Elements, Species, and Numbers"); 5) "Universalization et particularisation" ("Universalization and Particularization"); 6) "L'Individu comme espèce" ("The Individual as a Species"); and 7) "Le Temps retrouvé" ("Time Regained").

Based on studies of North American Indian tribes, the totemic studies identify two axes along which the myths and languages of totemic traditions can be classified: agricultural and hunting interests. The five other essays are concerned with mapping grids for totemic systems based on their symbolic significance.

The essay "Histoire et dialectique" ("History and Dialectic") in *La Pensée sauvage* engages Sartre in a debate about whether the "dialectical method" is properly employed in ethnological research. Lévi-Strauss maintains that since "the savage mind totalizes"[16] in its tendency to be anecdotal and geometrical, it is appropriate to use analytical reason in the service of the dialectical method. He portrays Sartre as raising the discipline of history to a preeminent position in the social sciences while disparaging the value of scientific method. Lévi-Strauss inverts that order and presents history as the starting point rather than the endpoint of intelligibility.

3. *Le Totémisme aujourd'hui* (1962). This book is more obviously united around a single theme than the others published during this period. It is a collection of essays about "totemism" as an artificial invention by anthropologists. This monograph makes a case for totemism as another form of myth-making whose structure has been ritualized by various societies. The "illusion" of totemism can be appreciated by studying the organic reality of its practice from the inside rather than from the outside perspective of the "civilized mind."

4. *La Voie des masques* (1975). Apparently listening to critics who complained about the heterogeneous nature of the essays in many of his books, Lévi-Strauss organizes his writings around a single motif once again. This time he analyzes ceremonial masks and their relationships to rituals in Indian tribes of the Northwest section of North America, particularly British Columbia and Alaska. Since he was involved in collecting these masks when he worked for the French Embassy in Washington and as a Curator for the Musée de l'Homme, he developed an interest in their use. He links the masks to myths which explain their supernatural function or origin within the rituals of tribes. The components of the masks are examined for their commentary on the relative values of plastic constituents within a certain geographical area.

5. *Le Regard éloigné* (1983). Dedicated to the memory of Roman Jakobson, who died in 1982, this collection of twenty-three essays, many of them previously published as freestanding articles, is supposed to demonstrate how "contemporary anthropology en-

deavors to discover and formulate systematic laws in several aspects
of human thought and activity."[17] His reference to "systematic laws"
applies to those patterns he himself found in kinship systems and
elsewhere to provide a role for the anthropologist as being able to
bridge the apparent contradiction between the unity of the human
spirit and the variety of cultural differences throughout the world.
The tone of this book impresses a politically and socially involved
role for the ethnologist.

The essays are divided into five divisions: 1) "L'Inné et l'acquis"
("The Innate and the Acquired")—one essay on race and culture,
the other warning about research in sociobiology; 2) "Famille, mar-
iage, parenté"—four essays variously treating family, marriage, and
familial relationship as issues in anthropology; 3) "Le Milieu et ses
représentations"—five essays about ambience relating ecology, empiricism, linguistics, language (based on an unpublished text by
Saussure on mythology as an act of naming), and sociology to structural anthropology; 4) "Croyances, mythes et rites" ("Beliefs, Myths,
and Rites")—six essays involving motifs of schizophrenia, forget-
fulness, Greek mythology, and twins in North American Indian
myths and an analysis of Apollinaire's poem "Les Colchiques"; and
5) "Contrainte et liberté" ("Constraint and Freedom")—two reflections on painting, one on the work of Max Ernst, the other on the
work of Anita Albus; a memoir of his life in New York City in
1941; and two essays on social problems, one on the creative child,
the other on the impossibility of legislating freedom and the concomitant need for tolerance.

Myths and More Myths

1. "La Structure des mythes" in *Anthropologie structurale*
(1958). Originally written in English, this article was published
in 1955 and then translated into French by Lévi-Strauss for this
anthology. Myth is observed to be both in language and beyond it
because of three properties peculiar to myth: 1) the meaning of myth
is found in the combination of components rather than in the isolated
components themselves; 2) the language of myth integrates myth
into its unique order; 3) this unique order is more complex than
mere linguistic expression. This last property leads him to distinguish poetic from mythical works. In mythical works, repetition
makes the structure of the works evident by revealing the *mythemes*

in the works. *Mythemes* are discrete components ("paquets de relations") of myths whose harmony with other mythemes accounts for the unique order of myths.

2.   "Comment meurent les mythes" ("How Myths Die") in *Anthropologie structurale,* 2 (1973).   Published initially as an article in a festschrift for Raymond Aron in 1971, this essay traces the transformation of myths into three other types of storytelling. He claims that a "principle of conservation" retains the "mythical framework" even though the form changes. The three types are legend, romantic narrative, and political ideology. These transformations legitimize history by lending both retrospective and prospective views to mythical structures.

3.   *Mythologiques* (1964–71).   The four-volume series entitled *Mythologiques* was subtitled as an Introduction to a Science of Mythology. The four volumes included 1) *Le Cru et le cuit (The Raw and the Cooked)* (1964), 2) *Du miel aux cendres (From Honey to Ashes)* (1966), 3) *L'Origine des manières de table (The Origin of Table Manners)* (1968), and 4) *L'Homme nu (The Naked Man)* (1971). All four volumes contain indexes of the myths and the originating tribes, and a bibliography. No single method or single mythology of the myths of North and South American Indian tribes results from these volumes. Instead, Lévi-Strauss provides patterns and motifs by which one could arrive at a single science of mythology, if that is desirable.

a) *Le Cru et le cuit* uses a Bororo myth from central Brazil about a bird-nester as the basis for constructing a rigorous network of axioms and postulates relating myths one to another. The title comes from the inversion of the Bororo myth by the Ge tribe into a myth relating to the cooking of food. In order to explain the nonobvious ties between these and other groups of myths, Lévi-Strauss uses the analogy of musical scores to speak about the nontemporal, serialized ties among these rules which are not imitative of some external reality. The musical series is almost a model for Lévi-Strauss in that the links of its components make little sense without the whole. Similarly, he ties together the harmony of 187 myths from sixty-eight American Indian tribes through abstract concepts and then groups them into diverse "schémas" (diagrams). The aim is to substantiate the existence of a common human spirit.

b) *Du miel aux cendres* centers its clustering of myths around the opposition between honey and tobacco. The diagrams involve com-

plicated axes positioning groups of myths in variations of the opposition between honey and tobacco. There are 265 myths from
sixty-five American Indian tribes included in these abstract "schémas." Although he insists throughout that these structural analyses
do not reject history, he nevertheless relates these myths with a
sweeping disregard for "the power and the lifelessness of the historical event."[18]

c) *L'Origine des manières de table* focuses upon how the codes of
table manners and meal recipes of individual societies are reflections
of how people see themselves and their world from within these
societies. These discussions and charts are based on 174 myths added
to a repertoire of seventy-seven used in the two previous volumes.
The myths are representative of ninety-two North or South American
Indian tribes.

Two of the presentations are especially significant for their in-
genious commentaries on lifestyles: 1) "Le Voyage en pirogue de la
lune et du soleil" ("The Canoe-Ride from the Moon and the Sun")
and 2) "La Balance égale" ("The Balancing Scale"). "Le Voyage" is
noteworthy for the cosmic plan of relating codes or motifs within
a system of relationships. Five codes are understood to be interwoven
in these myths: the astronomical, the geographical, the anatomical,
the sociological, and the ethical. Lévi-Strauss's chart juxtaposing
these codes is intriguing in its ingenuity. The second essay compares
and contrasts the ways arithmetic is presented in myths.

d) *L'Homme nu* begins with a reference to one of Lévi-Strauss's
colleagues, Edmund Leach, who applauded this series for bringing
respectability to comparative studies. The apparent reason for this
reference is to argue that he is doing this work to show how, and
not why, there are similarities between the myths of the North and
South American Indian tribes. Two hundred eighty-four new myths
are added to those of the first three volumes to represent 115 different
tribes. He returns to the bird-nester myth from the Bororo Indians
to isolate variants of that myth. When it becomes obvious that the
813 myths in the four-volume series do not provide a single unifying
pattern, Lévi-Strauss returns to the analogy begun in volume 1,
that of the musical series. Both mythology and music appear to be
forms without meaning. Upon further scrutiny, however, one can
discover their organic structure and transformation.

4. *L'Identité* (1977). These are the proceedings of a seminar
on the motif of "identity" directed by Claude Lévi-Strauss at the

Collège de France in 1974–75. Noteworthy contributors include Jean-Marie Benoist (one of his students whose work he much admires), Michel Serres, and Julia Kristeva, among others. "Identity," as that indefinable part of the self not communicable to others and that by which others know anyone, generates discussion as well as lectures from these philosophers, ethnologists, psychologists, mathematicians, linguists, and psychoanalysts. Lévi-Strauss, for his part, attests to the difficulty of translation while also rejecting what he calls "un nouveau obscurantisme" (a new obfuscation) by refusing to elaborate ties between peoples when possible.

5. *La Potière jalouse* (1985) (The jealous potter-woman). An anthology of myths generated from a Jivaro Indian (Peruvian) story about the origin of the world. The Sun and Moon were once married to Aôho, who followed the Moon into the sky with a basket of pottery-making clay. The Moon wanted to be rid of her and separated earth from sky, thus causing Aôho to fall to earth with her clay spread throughout the soil. She was also transformed into a nighthawk (whippoorwill). Fourteen untitled chapters of this book are devoted to variations on this myth. Chapter 13 has some theoretical discussions about the nature of myth, the plurality of mythical codes, and the dialectical relationships between the content and the form of myths. The last several pages of the final chapter (14) discuss the nature of "meaning" according to Lévi-Strauss. Basically, he proposes that meaning is in a relationship with, rather than contained in, any single element of a myth.

On the Inside Looking Out

At about the time of his debates with Jean-Paul Sartre subsequent to 1960, Lévi-Strauss understood himself to be the exponent of "structuralism" within ethnology. Despite the self-aggrandizement and self-promotion of these efforts, he did become a major theoretican of "structuralism," largely because of the wide readership of the following works.

1. *Anthropologie structurale* (1958). A collection of essays, this book constituted a particularly charged statement of his affinity with "structuralism." He provides essays linking anthropology with linguistics, myths, symbolism, and teaching. This work piqued Jean-Paul Sartre to defend philosophy in the face of what he understood to be a compromise on the part of Lévi-Strauss toward scientific method.

In the essay "Structure et dialectique," Lévi-Strauss claims that there is a dialectical relation between ritual and myth, which is inherently structural. This argument then claims "structural dialectics" to be an instrument of historical determination. Sartre's rebuttal of these "dialectics" will be discussed later in my presentation.

Anthropologie structurale is organized according to five major headings: 1) "Langage et parenté" ("Language and Kinship"); 2) "Organisation sociale" ("Social Organization"); 3) "Magie et religion" ("Magic and Religion"); 4) "Art" ("Art"); and 5) "Problèmes de méthode et d'enseignement" ("Problems of Method and Teaching"). The essay "Place de l'anthropologie dans les sciences sociales et problèmes posés par son enseignement" ("The Place of Anthropology in the Social Sciences and Problems Raised in Teaching It") promotes the international situation of social anthropology as an independent discipline within universities along with laboratory, museum, and research support appropriate to its interdisciplinary setting relating linguistics, sociology, archeology, psychology, and geography.

Another significant essay in *Anthropologie structurale* is "Le Sorcier et sa magie" ("The Sorcerer and His Magic"). Therein he reveals the power of witch doctors through their psychological control of the system of magic, understood by Lévi-Strauss as a language structure.

2. *Entretiens avec Lévi-Strauss.*   In the *Entretiens avec Lévi-Strauss* (1961), Georges Charbonnier interviews Lévi-Strauss and elicits from him explanations about the development of structuralism through the French ethnologist. These interviews were conducted for the French television station France 3 and aired during the period October to December 1959. Prior examples of ethnological research influenced Lévi-Strauss's decision to do ethnological and ethnographical work. The American anthropologist Robert Lowie became a model of the objectivity of the observer despite personal opinions about the moral consequences of certain cultural practices. Lowie studied the American Crow and Hopi Indians and produced exemplary monographs about them despite his disagreement with Hopi prayers for tribal afflictions as a punishment for personal wrongdoing.

The interviews are divided into nine chapters whose titles indicate the gist of the discussions: 1) "L'Ethnologue parmi nous" ("The Anthropologist and the Public"); 2) "Primitifs et civilisés" ("Primitive Peoples and 'Civilized' Peoples"); 3) "Horloges et machines à vapeur" ("Clocks and Steam Engines"); 4) "Les Niveaux d'authenticité" ("Levels of Authenticity"); 5) "L'Art et le groupe" ("Art and the Group"); 6) "Trois Différences" ("Three Differences" [between art in primitive and art in civilized societies]); 7) "De l'art comme système de signes" ("Art as a System of Signs"); 8) "Les Exigences du code" ("The Demands of the Code" [in art]); and 9) "Culture et langage" ("Culture and Language"). His basic tenet in these talks is that the origins of language are linked with the origins of culture. Language is understood here as the broad manifestation of human beings to communicate one with another.

3. *Anthropologie structurale,* 2 (1973). Another anthology of essays contains articles originally written in French or English and published elsewhere before and after volume 1. Four divisions organize the book into the past and future of anthropology, theoretical and practical discussions of kinship and social organization, mythology and ritual, and "progress" and the social sciences.

Regarding the past and future of anthropology, there are several key essays, some of which are no longer in print. "Le Champ de l'anthropologie" ("The Scope of Anthropology") is the lecture otherwise published in 1970 as the *Leçon inaugurale.* Two essays are devoted to his predecessors, one to Jean-Jacques Rousseau, the other to Emile Durkheim. Another article discusses why he changed the name of his chair at the Collège de France from Social Anthropology (originating with Marcel Mauss in 1938) to Comparative Religions of Nonliterate Peoples.

In Part 3 on mythology and ritual, three essays are significant. Two articles are concerned with specific myths from North American Indian tribes and have become identified with him for his analyses of them, the Asdiwal Story and the Four Winnebago Myths. Another essay is important for his explanations of the distinctions between his use of "structure" and Vladimir Propp's application of "form." This is the subject of my chapter 3.

In the section on the social sciences, he discusses the relationships among literature, the fine arts, and urban living. He also continues his presentation of "race and history" with an expansion of his 1952 essay. In this version, he introduces the issue of the role of progress in the "static history" of primitive societies and the need for the coalition of civilized societies (those included in the "progressive" notion of "cumulative history") for the promotion of "dynamic tolerance," the ongoing recognition of diversity he continues to advocate.

4. *Myth and Meaning* (1979). This is a collection of talks broadcast in English in December 1977 on the CBC Radio series "Ideas." The talks were assembled from a series of lengthy interviews between Claude Lévi-Strauss and Carole O. Jerome, producer of the Paris bureau of CBC. These talks are called the 1977 Massey Lectures and were basically replies to five series of questions.

These five series were organized into chapters entitled as follows: 1) "The Meeting of Myth and Science"; 2) " 'Primitive' Thinking and the 'Civilized' Mind"; 3) "Harelips and Twins: The Splitting of a Myth"; 4) "When Myth Becomes History"; and 5) "Myth and Music." Lévi-Strauss spoke in English replying to the following questions, which I have reduced to certain clusters and organized by chapter reference: 1) What is structuralism? Is it necessary to have order and rules to have meaning?; 2) Is "primitive" thought simply wrong by comparison with "scientific" thought? 3) Is humanity capable of focusing more on its similarities than on its differences? 4) How does the ethnologist avoid imposing order on myths? How do history and myth differ? 5) How do myth and music relate to one another and differ as languages? Generally, he responds with theoretical pronouncements about structuralism. In his chapter 4, he clearly distinguishes history as an open system with infinite possibilities whereas mythology is a closed system in that series of stories do compose clearly coherent, static, and recurring patterns.[19]

5. *Paroles données* (1984). This anthology of his lectures at the Collège de France and the École Pratique des Hautes Études provides insights into the beginnings of his books. Since he was required to offer a new course each semester at the Collège de France, he began the topics for his books with generalized hypotheses to his classes. We see in this work the questions he asked himself prior to writing each of his books. The essays are not long and often appear to be the results of course outlines during the practice of his thirty-two years teaching in Paris at the École Pratique des Hautes Études (from 1951 to 1960 as the Director of Studies in Comparative Religions for Non-Literate Peoples) and the Collège de France (from 1960 to 1982 in the chair of Social Anthropology). Five chapters devoted to the courses at the Collège de France are arranged the-

matically: 1) "Le Champ de la recherche" ("The Scope of Research"); 2) "Mythologiques"; 3) "Recherches sur la mythologie et le rituel"; 4) "Débats en cours sur l'organization sociale et la parenté" ("Ongoing Debates About Social Organization and Kinship"); 5) "Clan, Lignée, Maison" ("Clan, Bloodline, and Family Tree"). Each chapter has subtitles referring to the written works published by Lévi-Strauss as a result of these early questions. The sixth and last chapters contain nine résumés of courses given at the École Pratique des Hautes Études. These are thematically organized according to his interests in American Indian myths, marriage taboos, dualism, attitudes about souls, and the ritualized search for eagles among disparate peoples.

Chapter Two
Neo-Cartesian Lessons
The Fear of Being Alone

Claude Lévi-Strauss has devoted his entire ethnological career to doing research about how the human spirit functions. He did not begin with a tabula rasa, however. His basic assumption was that "we are prisoners of subjectivity."[1] Then he set about investigating the universal aspects of that subjectivity within all humanity. To reveal this universality would be to justify his own need for belonging to, or being a part of others. He had known difference himself and indeed remarked from his own experience that "something which can be true from inside a culture is no longer true when we try to consider it from the outside."[2] His own personal isolation was a case in point. Therefore, the univocal truth of empirical science had to be revealed to be only one logic among many. The dialectic of inside/outside in fact provided Lévi-Strauss with a model, one derived from the phenomenological camps so popular during his education at the Sorbonne, for analyzing other cultures, and especially their storytelling (or "mythmaking," as he called it).

Some of his critics[3] have taken him to task for the diverse logics of the myths he has analyzed. And yet the plural logics could be considered the true strength of his methodology. In contrast to a single tracking of the human spirit, the multiple paths recovered by Lévi-Strauss lead us to an appreciation of differentiation despite the common principles upon which intellectual diversity is based. The most basic of these common principles is choice. Whereas computer technology has taught us that even artificial language uses opposition in its application of Boolean logic (for example, 0 and 1 in eight-particle bits) to set up sophisticated programs, Lévi-Strauss allegedly discovered among the most remote cultures on earth a "Cartesian reduction which can only be practiced today in the most different and distant of settings."[4] Yet he revealed that even the human minds least acquainted with Western civilization operated according to binary distinctions. In volume 4 of his *My-*

thologiques, he insisted that binary discrimination is basic to any form of communication.[5]

This observation is a sequel to his remarks that contiguous peoples must distinguish themselves from one another and by so doing set up difference as a principle of identity. Politically, neighboring groups must then discover ways to bridge their distinctiveness and to translate their concerns to one another. The lack of recognizing the political consequences of not being translatable inspired Lévi-Strauss to write the UNESCO-funded pamphlet *Race et histoire,* decrying racism as a political and sociological manifestation of the monocultural tendencies of humanity. He would later remark in *Tristes tropiques* that "humanity lodges itself in monoculture and makes itself ready for the mass production of civilization like a beet."[6] He demonstrated no fondness for his own culture or civilization and sought differentiation as a catalyst for his analytical method.

Difference itself became, for Lévi-Strauss, the medium for recognizing order in the universe, an order in which dualities constitute the parameters for system. Some of his critics, such as Octavio Paz (*Lévi-Strauss—An Introduction,* Cornell University Press, 1970), concluded that the dualities revealed by Lévi-Strauss did not lead to understanding an intelligible cosmos, but in effect led to silence. However, Fredric Jameson noted well that, in the work of Lévi-Strauss, binary opposition is a "heuristic principle" which reveals the whole organizational basis for "the mythological hermeneutic."[7] In many ways binary differentiation operated dialectically for Lévi-Strauss, providing the polar parameters within which he proceeded with his analyses. Many of his analyses have revealed the nonconscious systems (i.e., hermeneutic per Jameson) of storytelling (i.e., mythologies per Lévi-Strauss) and thus suggest the unity of the human spirit which he had assumed from his earliest work.

Nevertheless, Lévi-Strauss identified and analyzed cultures distinct from his own and analyzed them through binary opposition. In this way, he demonstrated how apparent cultural differences mask a common base. But this common base is distinct from the racist imposition of homogeneity, which he called monocultural.

Instead, the bases identified by Lévi-Strauss pointed to the intellectual systems common within humanity rather than to the hegemonic imposition of common political or religious unanimity upon the mores of culturally distinct peoples. He himself noted that, whereas "dualistic organization is reduced to a method for the solution of certain problems in our social life,"[8] "structuralism refutes all dualism in that it is . . . the intimate union of the physical and the intellectual."[9] On the one hand, he relied upon the discrimination of data into neat polarities as his way of assessing order within the many foreign stories or "myths" he encountered in cultures distinct from his own. On the other hand, he concluded from his analyses that the systems thus discovered (leading him to postulate that a "structuralism" was possible) fused the apparent disparity between physical data apprehended by the senses and the intellectual evaluation of the links between the data.

Dualism vs. the Dialectic

Jean-Paul Sartre sponsored the publication of some essays by Lévi-Strauss in the journal *Les Temps modernes* during the 1950s. Sartre took exception, however, to the naive application of the binary or dualist "method." Although Lévi-Strauss insisted upon his Marxist inspiration and upon the compatibility of his dualist method with dialectical thinking,[10] Sartre was livid in his rejection of the emphasis upon system rather than upon the totality of Marxist praxis in the "structuralist method" developed by his colleague. An intellectual debate ensued which reminded some observers of the Scholastic argument about how many angels could dance on the head of a pin. Sartre rejected the analyses by Lévi-Strauss as examples of dialectical method and refuted any claims for Marxist inspiration in the binary methods employed by the ethnologist. Although Lévi-Strauss was very defensive about his dialectical method in search of a systematic analysis, he adapted his method only *after* the debate with Sartre and began deliberately using terminology that referred to the dialectic. For example, in the second volume of his *Anthropologie structurale* (1973), he noted that "the proof of the analysis is in the synthesis: if the synthesis cannot be realized, then the analysis remains incomplete."[11]

Despite all the posturing about whether Lévi-Strauss or Sartre understood the "proper" use of the dialectic for the intellectuals in Paris during the 1960s, Lévi-Strauss did learn from Sartre to use his binary method in the service of integration. From Trubetskoy's model (1933) of identifying "distinctive features" in linguistics with $+/-$, he adapted binary techniques of classifying "mythemes" (the elementary units in storytelling). Then Roman Jakobson (1941) influenced the application of the method to complex schemes such as metaphor/metonymy, acquired/nonacquired, and hosts of other oppositions not necessarily mutually exclusive. Jakobson and Lévi-Strauss collaborated on an analysis of Baudelaire's sonnet "Les Chats" in 1962 to demonstrate their "structuralist" application of this binary method. As Michael Riffaterre argued in his critique of their work,[12] it is a real question whether this "scientific" rigor contributes to an understanding of the complexities of the poem. Paul Ricoeur chimed in to criticize Lévi-Strauss for his "modern agnosticism"[13] in what was perceived as an antihumanistic method. But Lévi-Strauss reiterated his position that the binary method he espoused helped him to identify "the fundamental problem . . . of the relationship between an individual and the group, or, more precisely, between a certain kind of individual and certain demands of the group."[14] Although he had first stated this view in 1949, it was still pertinent in the early sixties because his social concern was humanistically based in its situation of the individual in society.

A Search for the Other

Lévi-Strauss espoused a dialogic method whose approach focused upon the symbiotic network of individual data-generating systems in their relationships. He refused naive dualistic approaches and developed complex (and complicated) ways to demonstrate the interaction of two apparently unrelated components in a myth or story. For example, he explained totemism as a "particular fashion of formulating a general problem, namely, how to make opposition, instead of being an obstacle to integration, serve rather than produce it."[15] Sartre's debate with him had reinforced his conviction to demonstrate the service of dialogue in generating a system linking unique data to an elaborately linked network. Mere dualism is the appearance whereas the juxtaposition of the obvious and the latent produce unsuspected harmonies in the storytelling process.

From his position, stated in *Tristes tropiques,* that any problem could be resolved by applying the same method of opposing two traditional views of the same problem,[16] he developed his method into a syntactical chain of forms such that the binary approach did not merely reveal motifs but also demonstrated the flow of the organizational process in storytelling. Vladimir Propp had shown

him in his "morphology of the folktale" (1927) how Russian formalism produced a static model for latent forms. Lévi-Strauss sought
instead a method that was dynamic in identifying the formal substrata of stories or myths.

His dynamic method revealed a sensitivity to the modulation that
links the various components of a story. In Baudelaire's sonnet "Les
Chats," for example, he and Jakobson maintained that "the com-
position of the whole work is based on the tension between two
kinds of arrangement, and between symmetrical and dissymmetrical
constituents."[17] This type of analysis assumed that there is a "glue"
holding together the components and that this glue can be identified. In addition, this glue is strung between polarities that are
usually not obvious.

These assumptions were not widely held and have elicited considerable criticism. Some opponents were amused by the "contrived
dyads"[18] of Lévi-Strauss and thought that the whole method was a
type of trick or chicanery without any profundity based on a semantic
account of the role of ambiguity in his binary play. Others saw the
Lévi-Strauss type of analysis as a serious threat because "one is as
much read 'by' it as a reader 'of' it."[19] In other words, we are being
written into this neo-Cartesian system by tacitly accepting its assumptions. There may very well be modulation in the rhythm of a
story, but it is not necessarily subject to a polarized model. Nevertheless, the tensions discovered by Claude Lévi-Strauss did lead him
into conjectures about the nature of the "glue" that caused the
human mind to link things together into identifiable stories. And
so he became the "structuralist" by adapting his method into a
philosophical attitude about an intelligible cosmos. His conception
of "structure" provided the cohesive view needed to link the polarized parameters of his initial analysis.

Chapter Three

Distinguishing Structure from Form

Form Is Not Enough

During the 1920s and 1930s, the Russian Formalists attracted considerable attention. The publication in 1928 of Vladimir Propp's *Morphology of the Folktale* heralded the era of formalist analysis. Lévi-Strauss contributed a preface to a translation of Propp's work and appeared, superficially, to be in tune with the abstract tone of the formalist program. His agenda, however, was quite distinct because, as an empirically based scientist, he believed that his work entailed knowledge of the most specific details of an ethnological project. He disputed Propp's attitude toward stories because the formalist analysis into functions did not satisfactorily explain the whole of a story. Lévi-Strauss could not so easily separate form from content and therefore sought a manner of explaining stories such that all the significant details were pieced together in a credible analysis. For him, a story entailed the narration of myths, religions, kinship systems, masks, and other cultural artifacts in which humanity had invested belief for its social identity. Form and content were not justifiably separable for Lévi-Strauss. He needed a holistic analytical method to explain the nature of the human spirit.

In his desire to account for all the elements of a given story, Lévi-Strauss sought a method which would be systematic in its analysis of all the parts of a whole. The system he preferred was modeled upon a biological view of "structure." There would be no separation of form from content. Instead, a vital, unifying map would account for the coherence of all the parts in a given story. Rather than divide and conquer, "structure" was to provide constituent analysis with a method and a model based on empirical findings. In his rebuttal of the formalist reliance on the separation of form from content, he indicated that meaning cannot be found in either one or the other, and argued that "it is only the way in which the different elements of the content are combined together which gives a meaning."[1]

In his striving for systematic internal order to give meaning or coherence to a story Lévi-Strauss focused upon the narration of a story to the exclusion of the historical, cultural, and ideological factors involved in the act of narrating. His critics have taken issue with the incompatibility of history with his type of structure. Paul Ricoeur went so far as to say that history provided "destructive disorder"[2] in the Lévi-Strauss system. In his defense, Lévi-Strauss did not pretend to situate these stories in a specific milieu.

His scheme entailed analyzing as many stories as possible to isolate their universal properties and thus to understand the human spirit better through its penchant for telling stories. Most of his "myths" or stories were collected from groups of people outside the mainstream of Western ideological and historical influences. Once again, by studying what is outside that which is commonly assumed to be history, Lévi-Strauss shifted the study of narration from its context or literary history to the internal dynamics of its "structure."

The "structure" would reveal the characteristics of a story's "system," according to Lévi-Strauss. He identified four latent properties to be discovered by the model of the "structure" as he conceived it: 1) all the facts of the story; 2) its predictable features; 3) the model's potential for transformation into another model of the same type; 4) the changing role of the elements in relation to one another.[3] These properties of the system in his models allowed for change but were not always obviously implemented, especially in his now classic diagrams, which appeared to convey static architectural schemes for the myths or stories being analyzed. Nevertheless, he insisted that the models were systematic and logical accounts of the "unsuspected harmonies" linking stories together. For example, his study of kinship systems revealed a reliance upon the "avuncular" network of relationships: the uncles were crucial structuring principles in how families narrate their own stories. He pointed out that the "avuncular" phenomenon must be "treated as a relationship interior to a system . . . which must be considered as a whole to appreciate its structure."[4] So "structure" and "system" were conceived together by Lévi-Strauss in his pursuit of a holistic method to analyze the human spirit's presence in storytelling.

In Search of Holism

In his pursuit of an internal logic to storytelling, Lévi-Strauss sometimes dazzled his readers with complex diagrams, apparently inspired by mathematics. This dazzling effect earned him the suspicion of other intellectuals regarding whether his logical "method" was empirically based at all. On the one hand, some anthropologists, such as Edmund Leach, were skeptical about the "structure" as something directly observable.[5] On the other hand, one of the most astute critics of Lévi-Strauss, Mireille Marc-Lipiansky, observed that his "structure" is a logical construct to make manifest that which is implicit.[6] Hence, the matter being considered is not observable in its raw data so that the empirical method may not always be appropriate for studying narration.

Lévi-Strauss maintained that, although the "structure" is intelligible upon its discovery, it develops in complexity a kind of "logical inertia or indifference."[7] He borrowed from the realm of mathematics a formulary reliance upon matrices and diagrams to map out the relationships in a story. This "map," or schematic, provided him with the blueprint of the "structure" whose laws and rules could then be isolated. But the rigorous logic of the "structure" appears lost in the schematics he constructed for the stories. And, indeed, there is more to structure than logic. In his enthusiasm to discover the implicit laws regulating signs and symbols, Lévi-Strauss was inspired by Richard Wagner's dictum from *Meistersinger:* "make up your own rules, but follow them."[8] Indeed, in order to account for the internal dynamics of storytelling, he constructed his own rules and applied them to the stories. Lévi-Strauss did not consciously impose an external order. Instead, he understood his work to be that of putting himself in congruence with the harmony of stories and then simply laying out the rules that were there.

In laying out these rules, he was also seeking the basic components of a structure's system. In his study of the elementary structures of kinship systems, he called the avuncular relationship "the authentic atom of kinship systems."[9] Around this "atom," he then discovered three principles by which the atom was structured: 1) the demands of the law; 2) reciprocity; and 3) the notion of the gift. The principles were not so important in themselves as they were in their networks of reciprocal natures. Lévi-Strauss was intent upon showing how these principles were governed by the energy of a narrative. This

energy, derived from human cultural systems, would be understood
once the rules of narrative functioning were isolated.

Plus c'est la même chose, plus ça . . .

On occasion, Lévi-Strauss did find a series of stories related one
to the other in some fashion. The "fashion" of their relationship
was organized around what he called a "sacred" or "magical" core
(*paquet*)[10] which allowed the stories to change shape, that is, be
transformed with various episodes, while also retaining a universal
appeal with similar systems.

The differences in appearances within some stories in fact con-
cealed similarities revealed by Lévi-Strauss with his studies of the
transformations from one myth to another. However, his schematics
for tracing the transformations were often so intricate that one won-
ders with Catherine Clément whether Lévi-Strauss can claim to be
a transmitter of these mythical transformations or an interpreter of
the myths or stories.[11] He identified ties for us among the various
myths he collected, but the connections between these myths may
not actually exist as historical influences of one story upon another.
Instead, his connections reveal psychological patterns about how
storytelling is a universally human means to construct meaning.
Some of his critics, such as Paul Ricoeur, throw their hands up in
frustration to see how Lévi-Strauss will sometimes make "sense out
of non-sense"[12] by rearranging the original story to provide coherence
where there appeared to be none. Others find that, despite some
drawbacks, the structural approach does allow Lévi-Strauss to "draw
conclusions"[13] about the meaning of stories and to relate that meaning to the larger realms of aesthetics and the psychology of the
storyteller.

Indeed, the "structure" of a story can relate its author and the
ideological system in which the story was narrated. Generally speaking, however, Lévi-Strauss was not interested in the contextual
analysis of a story. His purpose in theorizing and applying the
"structure" to a story was to give a holistic explanation to its internal
dynamics. He went into great detail while explaining the internal
autonomy of the components of a story, such that many historians,
psychoanalysts, ideologues, and others concerned with the affective
factors external to a story object to his dogmatic tone, which pre-
cludes their expansion of the "structure" of a story. His focus of

attention was upon what was said in the story and how the story-teller(s) used "intellectual handiwork" to express a whole repertoire of values perhaps unarticulated otherwise. In his enthusiasm to account for that repertoire, Lévi-Strauss did make a case for the role of change, transformation, in storytelling, specifically in the kind of story he called "myth." It is in the changing character of stories in myths that "contextualists" can adapt the "structure" of Lévi-Strauss to their methods.

Chapter Four
De-myth-ologizing
Translating and Interpreting

Among the stories analyzed by Claude Lévi-Strauss were narratives called myths. More than a simple series of narrated events, a myth is a narrative invested with belief by a group of individuals and expressed in varying ways by other cultures. Myth is a product of a social milieu, a sociolinguistic formulation of a story common to many cultures. When Lévi-Strauss encountered myths, he analyzed their linguistic reformulations as variants of a universal human spirit. He realized that "myth is the part of language where the formula *traduttore, traditorre* reaches its lowest truth value."[1] The translating implicit in the conveying of myth intrigued him, especially since he himself had been involved with translating his otherness to the French, himself from one culture to another, and his writings from one language to another. If myths realized the least amount of treachery (*traditorre*) as they are translated (*traduttore*), the implication for Lévi-Strauss was that there is a scale of values in the relationship between translation and treachery and that myth is the means to attain the lowest common denominator between the two. This mathematical term is no accident because Lévi-Strauss used formulas and equations to assemble the various stories he encountered.

The logic of mathematics could help him preclude losing information. He was preoccupied with the loss of information ensuing from translations of his work into various languages. Throughout his career, he has been overly defensive about his critics' misinterpreting him because of his writings in both French and English (of no small consequence is the American variation of English with which he had considerable contact during the period 1941–48). He often insisted that he thought in one language and expressed himself in another. Responding rather late in his career (1976) to what he observed to be a "new tendency toward obscurity" in ethnological studies, he admitted that "we can rightfully say that a translation is never perfect. . . ."[2] A certain "je ne sais quoi" or noise slips by as we try to move information from one register to another. And so it was not only with the information collected by Lévi-Strauss but also with his own narration, which gave form to the information after it had been collected.

Hence, Lévi-Strauss sought a manner of being able to share the essence of "humanity," despite the apparent differences in cultures and languages. In the different cultures with which he was acquainted in his early years (Belgian, French, Jewish), he noted the commonality of storytelling. In the remote cultures encountered during his early ethnological travels (the Bororo, Nambikwara, and Tupi-Kawahib Indians of the Mato Grosso in Brazil), the storytelling became an autobiographical means of translating information. Lévi-Strauss realized that "the very nature of a sign system was that it be transformable, in other words, 'translatable' into the language of another system with the help of permutations."[3] The "myths" he encountered appeared to give him the skeleton key to unlock various sign-systems because they provided the universal common denominator of storytelling. It then became a question of how to arrive at those permutations that would reduce to a minimum the loss attendant to translating.

Lévi-Strauss had been attracted to Jean-Jacques Rousseau as his historical antecedent, and learned many ethnological lessons from him. In *Tristes tropiques,* Rousseau was portrayed as being a slave to myth.[4] This insight had to do with Rousseau's antisocial behavior and his reluctance to see the socializing and humanistic influences of myth. In contrast, Lévi-Strauss realized that through studying myths and the rituals identified with them he could arrive at a "homology" (that is, a likeness in structure between different organisms having a common origin) or a "homomorphism" (that is, a superficial resemblance between organisms of different groups) of human nature.[5] In this way, he could utilize myth to study human nature rather than to isolate himself from it as Rousseau had done in the eighteenth century. Myth was to become the primary means for Lévi-Strauss to make his mark on ethnology. Through myth he could also integrate his personal concern with "otherness," that is, with how the apparent differences of peoples on the face of the earth relate to their common humanity at the core of life itself.

He discovered ever-so-subtle traits or structures for myths found among the most isolated cultures in the world and thus began to find the various types of logic linking these myths into mythologies.

His four-volume series *Mythologiques,* continued in *La Potière jalouse,*
is a testament to these types of logic. The patterns he discovered
in myths reaffirmed the role of rituals in history and stimulated,
despite the narrow view of some opponents to structuralist research,
a realignment of history and ethnology. In his inaugural lecture to
the chair of Social Anthropology at the Collège de France in 1960,
Lévi-Strauss noted this realignment: "The essence of myths . . . is
to revive a forgotten past, to apply it, like a grid, to the present
in order to discover here a meaning where the two faces of history
and structure coincide."[6]

This coincidence is found in the ability of myths to bring together
apparent contradictions of diachronic and synchronic orders, of the
linear succession of historical events and the logical, nongeometrical
associations of rituals (such as totemism, which Lévi-Strauss himself
studied intensively) to the meanings given to them by their practitioners. These apparent contradictions coalesce into the narrative
coherence of myths with such power that he has compared his
analyses of them to studies of musical scores.[7] Of course, some critics
have objected to the comparison of verbal and nonverbal media. But
the work of Lévi-Strauss must be understood in a semiotic context
whereby communication in general is observed for its commentary
on the otherness of the human condition. Instead, Miriam Glucksmann has pointed out that the issue of whether one or more logic(s)
are understood in myths by Lévi-Strauss is more significant.[8] If there
is a unity to the many myths he discovered, then his dream of
revealing the human spirit might be abetted by his research. If not,
then the haunting question of otherness returns in his work.

The Problem of the One and the Many

One might wonder why the myths from the Classical Greeks and
Romans are poorly represented within the mythologies studied by
Lévi-Strauss. He did stipulate that any myth consisted of all its
versions from any culture.[9] He has been criticized, however, for his
choice of myths, for selecting only those stories that fit into the
schema or formula he developed in advance. And yet he insisted
that his method was very different in its conception since he considered it legitimate to conduct "research from the inside, to mend
meaning together, except for the mending, the interpretation given
by philosophers and historians to their own mythology. . . ."[10]

He was opposed to the totalizing type of meaning implied by practitioners of disciplines who already understand systems of time and
thought prior to examining a myth. Instead, he believed it to be
intellectually honest to describe the innate order, or disorder, of
different myths or versions of myths as they existed cross-culturally.

Of course, there is value given to the logical ordering or plotted
coherence of myths. Lévi-Strauss was intent upon finding the common human spirit across the apparent heterogeneity of cultural
contexts. In fact, he went so far as to say that "the purpose of myth
is to provide a logical model capable of overcoming a (real) contradiction."[11] So one of the strengths of myths is to be able to outdo
logic by providing a Hegelian synthesis whose discursive strength
overcomes the trap of contradiction. It is this suggestion of Hegelian
"idealism" that has inspired the animosity of many of his intellectual
critics. There is almost a religious fervor in his belief that these
stories appeal to a higher order than that of human logic. It is
curious that Lévi-Strauss once took the position that religious fervor
was a kind of "ideal home where the ultimate synthesis could be
realized"[12] even though it never can be. It has never been obvious
that the synthesis promised either by religion in its perfect form or
by a restricted group of cohering myths in its imperfect form could
be realized either by Lévi-Strauss or by others. The ideal promised
by myths were individual variants of logic whose plural nature could
not be overcome despite his hope for a glimpse of our common
human spirit.

The Circular Discourse of Mythology

Assuming the unity of the human spirit prior to his research,
Lévi-Strauss examined myths to verify his postulate. And yet the
diagrams he invented to account for the universal properties are not
consistently similar. He insisted upon his discovery of the common
human spirit in myths shared by groups of peoples separated spatially
and temporally. Indeed some myths did have variations originating
in cultures that did not have obvious influences upon each other.
Octavio Paz noted that the research by Lévi-Strauss effectively portrayed myth as a sentence in a circular discourse whose repetition
and variation give it specifically different meanings.[13]

But Lévi-Strauss chose to focus upon the similarities rather than
the differences of the various myths he collected. Intent upon de-

veloping rather than repeating the obsessions of Rousseau, he noted, in volume 4 of his *Mythologiques,* the circle implied by his method: "the essence of every myth or group of myths is to forbid our imprisonment therein . . . ; one problem arises, and in order to solve it we have to get outside the circle traced by analysis."[14] The stories narrated by the myths are never closed or finite wholes in themselves. If there is circular structure to myths, the method of analyzing the myths a priori set it up and generated a paradigm within which they could be understood, that is, as indexes of the narrating power of our common humanity. There is also a threat within the assimilating power of the ethnologist bringing certain myths together and likewise discarding others: closure is imposed by the collector upon the structure of a corpus of myths,[15] thus precluding the very openness that is promised by the infinite choices available to a narrator intent upon storytelling.

Within the circle of certain restricted myths, Lévi-Strauss did portray how myths generate meaning. He would have myth as constituted primarily by language structured at the level of the grammatical sentence. Sentence structure provides the promise of an ideal: economy of explanation, the unity of solution, and the reconstruction of the whole from a fragment. These three goals of myth analysis justify Paul Ricoeur's criticism of Lévi-Strauss as a Kantian, that is, guiding the spirit of his method with a predisposed abstract plan. Each of the goals finds its elementary realization in the organization of grammar. First, the economy of explanation is found in the totalizing power of grammar to provide verbal relationships that literally retrace the power of the human spirit. This power integrated human nature and culture together in an anecdotal, rather than a dialectical, explanation of the world. Second, the unity of solution was found in the basic coherence of the sentence. This grammatical unit was also the elementary semantic unit for narration in a given tribe or group of people and thus literally predicated and verbalized the cosmology of the people and concomitantly of the human mind. For example, the Oedipus myth is a story about someone (Oedipus) answering an unanswerable riddle (of the Sphinx). This social situation is narrated in sentences, each one developing the tragedy of the human family while also verifying the riddle about the origins of human life. Did the first human being come from man and woman or was the first human being born from the earth? This cosmological riddle is addressed by the social predicament of Oedipus, according to Lévi-Strauss. Third, sentence structure allowed the reconstruction of the whole from a fragment because of the dependence of human meaning upon the elementary constituent units of the sentence. So Lévi-Strauss analyzed myths geometrically by tracing the evolution of mythical variants from a certain elemental story, modified by the human mind in its various cultural contexts throughout history and the world. Indeed, he did tell us that the story narrated by myths is not a closed one. Despite his formulas and analyses suggesting the opposite, the 811 myths collected as volume 4 of his *Mythologiques* point to the open-ended nature of the variants yet to be found, even after his *La Potière jalouse* (1985).

Myth as a Psychological Crucible

A basic disparity exists in the structural analysis of myths for Lévi-Strauss between understanding and narrating myth. In his two most widely renowned analyses of myths (the Oedipus myth[17] and the story of Asdiwal),[18] he divided the stories into segments and then charted their gross constituent units to explain the social and cosmological commentaries implied thereby. For example, the story of Oedipus is understood by him as divisible into eleven segments organized into a chart with four columns. To narrate the myths using these segments, one can read the chart either from top to bottom or from left to right. The variance in the readings produces a similar effect to that of the variants in the Oedipus myth. Michael Polanyi has observed that, although Lévi-Strauss claimed to have discovered the mechanical process of thought inherent in the physical structure of matter, the charts produced by the French ethnologist as evidence were only "a crude approximation of the actual process of acquiring knowledge."[19] Rather than epistemological acuity, however, the Lévi-Strauss analyses of myths give us psychological perceptions into how the human mind translates its struggle with its natural ("nature" for Lévi-Strauss) environment and its social predicament ("culture").

As he collected myths from various peoples throughout the world, he became known as an "armchair ethnologist" spending most of his time sifting through and digesting the results of field work done by others. Consequently, Lévi-Strauss the writer, especially in his role as an adapter of the analytical traditions of structuralist lin-

guistics, was often relegated to the epistemological realm of philosophy. Rather than earning respect as an anthropologist, he earned
renown for his philosophical insights into epistemology from his
studies of cultural artifacts,[20] especially since Michel Foucault's concerns with "epistemes"[21] were also popularly given the misnomer
of "structuralist." Foucault, Roland Barthes, Jacques Lacan, and
Lévi-Strauss were all conveniently grouped together in popular intellectual circles as "structuralists." But this tag did little to enhance
the understanding of the independent evolution of their works.

As an epistemologist, Lévi-Strauss was especially valuable for his
perceptiveness about the workings of the human psyche and how it
translated common human concerns into cultural artifacts. The "psychology" he discovered in myths transcends the social parameters
of a given group and the epistemic qualifications of a certain intellectual paradigm. The vision he had of this psychology was characteristic of humanity in general, of what he called the human spirit,
the essence of our humanity. Indeed, he believed that "if the human
spirit appears determined right down to its myths, then 'a fortiori'
it must be so determined throughout."[22] In this reflection, he indicated his observation that mythical constructs were close to the
very core of the human spirit. But there is no individual human
being expressing a solipsistic concern through a myth. Lévi-Strauss
realized that myths "form the discourse of a specific society . . .
a discourse for which there is no individual transmitter."[23] Nor do
we get from him a sociological tract about what a group of myths
tells us about a certain collective of peoples united by their similar
narratives. Lévi-Strauss had a much larger vision of the collectivity
behind mythmaking.

The Family of Myths

The myths collected by Lévi-Strauss belong to a sort of collective
unconscious, almost Jungian in its psychological universality.
Whereas the French ethnologist noted that all variants of a single
story were his subject, he also insisted that all myths were, in a
way, variants of one another, translations of similar concerns within
the human spirit. In a 1966 interview,[24] he noted that, in order to
understand a "single" myth, one had to be aware of how it was
translated from a different myth. Later, in his *Mythologiques,* he
elaborated this idea, stating that "every myth is by its very nature

a translation and . . . originates in another myth from a neighboring but foreign people."[25] The "neighboring" proximity does not have to be a geographical one. Psychological families also exist, uniting apparently divergent ("foreign") interests in their myths. Certainly, Lévi-Strauss was not content to analyze the appearances of heterogeneity on the surfaces of the stories. Instead, he explored meanings beneath, or at least not obvious, in the mere synopsis of a myth.

Why go beyond the surface? What led Lévi-Strauss to believe that there was any sort of reality other than the one uniting the subject matter? He was inspired by Freud's explorations of the unconscious, Chomsky's theory of "deep structure" in transformational grammar, the manifold dualities in structural linguistics, among other influences, to suspect that the stories narrated by peoples throughout the world had so much in common that they must reflect a unity of motivation, a common bond transcending the political and prejudicial differences separating families and even nations. He, too, was haunted throughout his life by these very differences, which kept him from being "recognized" until the appearance of *Tristes tropiques* in 1955. That common bond, that gluey matter, was not easily recognized, even by Lévi-Strauss himself. He was accused, as I have indicated previously, of identifying many kinds of logic operating within various groups of myths. At one point, however, he did bring together several observations that approximate the unity in myths: "We know, in fact that myths are transformed . . . in space. The transformations thus respect a kind of conservation principle of mythical matter. . . ."[26] It is those very "transformations" that bring me now to a discussion of how this "structuralist" ethnologist was antistructuralist in his very application of the principles of structuralist linguistics to myths. Through his "Kantian" postulate of the "conservation principle of mythical matter," he sought a way to link the diversity in the content of myths. In that pursuit, he prepared the way for the transition from structuralist taxonomies to semiotic explanations of human communication.

Chapter Five
The Generation of Transformation
The Heart of the Matter

Although he has long been identified with bringing "structural linguistics" into ethnology, the "structuralist" label has hampered the appreciation of many key concepts in the research by Claude Lévi-Strauss. "Structuralist" implies a timeless, fixed way of looking at reality. His twenty-year struggle with myths and their universal presence, however, made him realize that structure is derived from observations on transformations. In an interview for *Magazine littéraire* in 1985, he defined "structure" as "a system which remains identical through transformations."[1] Hence, there is a substratum to his "structures" whereby one can account for changes in appearances and their movement through time and space. This role of change in his research has not been so obvious to his readers over the years. "Structuralism" has been frequently discounted because of its orientation toward a reductionist, formulaic presentation of a story. Such an orientation appears to preclude a historical context accounting for development and change. But it must be noted that Lévi-Strauss did not intend to dismiss change but preferred instead to present how change takes place and what the metamorphosis looks like when examined across time and space.

From his early work on the cross-cultural prohibition of incest, he discovered that the apparent pattern of the incest taboo was based upon an unsuspected commerce: the monopoly of women. This insight has brought his work to the attention of feminist thinkers, including Simone de Beauvoir and Jane Gallop, to mention prominent examples from the French and American camps. As de Beauvoir noted in her review of his *Structures élémentaires de la parenté* (1947), Lévi-Strauss demonstrated through his study of incest that the problem was especially revealing in the treatment of cousins descended from a brother and sister ("cousins croisés"), rather than uniquely from either brothers or sisters, because in that relationship cousins were treated differently in order to direct the woman to another social group: "Cross-bred cousins, that is, descended from a brother and a sister, come from families who are in an antagonistic position to each other, in a dynamic imbalance that only marriage can resolve."[2]

Thus, the woman became a commodity to enable the families of her cousins to resolve the differences arising from the birth of children differing in sex. The incest taboo was a convenient means to control the destiny of women and their families. Gallop would later proclaim that "Lévi-Strauss's formulation of this general system of exchange is structuralism's major contribution to feminist theory."[3] Thus the French ethnologist was able to study such a profoundly common human story as that prohibiting incest and trace the metamorphosis of a common result throughout history and across cultures: the commercial exploitation of women through social coding.

This phenomenon was observed not as mere flux, as simple change wrought upon history through the incest taboo, but rather as the metamorphosis of a common human practice. It is no coincidence that Lévi-Strauss made a case for ethnology as one of the social sciences. In France, the discipline is appropriately grouped with the "human sciences" ("les sciences humaines"), given the concern Lévi-Strauss expressed about identifying the human spirit through this "science." In chapter 10, I will discuss his contributions to the "humanities" as the English-speaking world understands these areas of study. Suffice it to say at this point that he addressed the "humanness" of humanity with what he called "a 'transformational' rather than a 'fluxional' method."[4] It is this method of identifying the "transformations" that concerns us here.

Claude Lévi-Strauss had a knack for identifying systems of relationships between apparently unique phenomena in a social context. I have already spoken about his propensity for seeing structures and myths in cross-cultural patterns. An abiding aim in these studies has been identified by Fredric Jameson as "the mechanisms of transformation by which the mythical structure is recombined or articulated into its various utterances or versions. . . ."[5] Lévi-Strauss certainly had an abiding (and to some of his readers, annoying) interest in the utility of algebraic equations, musical scores, binary functions similar to the phonemically distinctive features identified by the Prague School linguist Trubetskoy, and diagrammatic schemes

for charting apparently isolated items such as the use of masks by
"primitive" peoples. Of course, these "mechanisms" reveal the pov-
erty of the empirical method in not being able to come to terms
with transformation. As one of his readers pointed out, "in strictly
anthropological terms, he recognized the failure to realize that structure is not to be found at the empirical level, but that it is superimposed on the social facts."[6]

On the other hand, the superimposition of some sort of mechanism
to account for the transformation of the "human spirit" into various
historical and cultural settings has some drawbacks in its differentiation from empirical data. Lévi-Strauss and Roman Jakobson collaborated on a "structuralist" (mainly inspired by the Prague School's
phonemic analyses) reading of Charles Baudelaire's poem "Les Chats"
published in 1961. The reading claimed to be an example of the
scientific analyses promised by structuralist linguistics for literary
criticism. This essay enfuriated many literary sensibilities by exemplifying T. S. Eliot's wariness of "the lemon-squeezer school of
criticism"[7] and consequently generated considerable debate about
the utility of "structuralist" methods for literary criticism. One
opponent, Michael Riffaterre, objected that "the analytical categories applied can pull together under one label phenomena which
are in fact totally different from one another in the poetic structure."[8]
For example, the feminine rhyme scheme in the poem by Baudelaire
was explained independently of its poetic context. As a result, the
"mechanisms" of transformation chosen by Lévi-Strauss produced
changes which were not always felicitous and which sometimes
provoked disharmony, internally and externally, rather than explain
the internal coherence of the artifact.

"Translater" and Translating

The disharmony provoked by Lévi-Strauss reminds us of the crucial problem in his work: the relationships of insider to outsider.
These relationships, in social and cultural contexts, can be understood within the scope of cultural assimilation, social distinctiveness,
and racism. For the ethnologist, these issues provide opportunities
for wrestling with how and when to translate differences and when
to recognize the role of noise, the "je ne sais quoi" to be respected
for its integrity in a given social group. The ethnologist is not

usually a native of the group being studied, so he or she is thus better able to respect difference rather than to judge it, or assimilate it, thereby compromising its integrity.

One consequence of not having spent much time doing fieldwork as an ethnologist was that the subject being discussed was dependent upon someone else's witness. Hence, except for his work on Brazil and a trip to East Pakistan, displacement (in French, *translater*) was a condition inherent to the writings of Lévi-Strauss and influential in the role of transformation in his research. As I have already noted, he was very sensitive about the problems of his writing in both French and English. Readers often find him saying that "a translation is never perfect."[9] And yet translation was at the heart of his activity as a writing ethnologist. If his translating activity was not logically "tight" with its loopholes for the "je ne sais quoi," what was his translating activity all about?

Indeed, Lévi-Strauss understood all ethnology to be involved in the transformational work at the heart of all translating. The task of the ethnologist was to respond to the question of what does all this mean and "in order to answer it, we are obliged to 'translate,' in our language system, rules primitively given in a different language system."[10] He repeated (as he often republished his articles in book-length collections) this same insight in his inaugural lecture for the Social Anthropology chair at the Collège de France in 1960 so its importance for him cannot be denied. Once again Lévi-Strauss projected his own personal concern for difference and its acceptance within the realm of ethnology. In this regard, he published a UNESCO-commissioned treatise in 1952 entitled *Race et histoire* (revised in *Le Regard éloigné,* 1983), which promoted tolerance on an international scale.

The translation of rules is a semiotic activity capable of revealing our humanity found in the transformations involved in communication. Lévi-Strauss was acquainted with the work of the American pioneer in semiotics, C. S. Peirce, who understood a "sign" to be that which replaces something for someone. The act of linguistic replacement (and displacement) had a special importance for the French ethnologist in his study of various myths, family structures, and totemism because these phenomena were sign systems for him. It was no accident that he recognized the role of metamorphosis within these systems. He would have us recognize with him that "the self-identity of sign systems is being transformable, that is 'translatable,' into the language of another system, with the help of permutations."[11]

Inside the Looking Glass

His study of the "permutations" resulting from translating cultures one to another led Lévi-Strauss to a life-long passion for systems of exchange. These systems, examined under the inspiration of Marcel Mauss—his predecessor at the Collège de France renowned for his seminal study of cross-cultural gift-giving—revealed affinities in the networks among kinship, economics, and language. His own personal crisis of the relationship between insiders and outsiders led him from the discovery of the exchange of women in kinship systems to an investigation of a "dialogue" with psychoanalysis in search of a common denominator for the permutations of kinship, economic, and language exchange systems. The nonconscious arena (see chapter 9) offered a viable crucible for the discrepancies observed in the appearances (for example, the incest taboo) of exchange systems.

Lévi-Strauss began to appreciate these systems as human lines of demarcation to differentiate, psychologically, various groups within a cultural community. In his study of masks used by socially isolated tribes, he noted that conscious designs are not exclusive lines of demarcation for understanding cultural artifacts: "Similar to a myth, a mask denies as much as it affirms; it is not constituted only by what it says or what it claims to say, but by what it excludes."[12] Hence, Lévi-Strauss was intrigued by seeing the appearances of exchange as superficial disguises for systems lurking beneath the surface.

Consequently, Lévi-Strauss developed an affinity for disciplines, such as psychoanalysis, that provided methods for probing the disparity between appearance and substance. The philosophical distinctions between conscious and unconscious, recessive and dominant features (Trubetskoy's phonemic analyses), and surface structure/deep structure (Chomsky's transformational linguistics) helped to reinforce his methodological choices in search of underlying systems. In fact, his search was based on the assumption of a unified human spirit behind these plural systems.

When asked about the nature of "the primitive mind" ("la pensée sauvage"), he answered that it was "the system of postulates and axioms necessary to establish a code permitting us to translate, in the least harmful way, 'the other' into 'ours' and reciprocally. . . ."[13] Notice that he preferred to label the basic human soul as reducible to "the system" definable in mathematical terms.

Although many of his readers have relegated his thought to intellectual, abstract terms sometimes defined as mathematical, I would like to be even more precise and claim a geometrical sensitivity in Claude Lévi-Strauss. For example, he has been especially intent, toward the end of his career, to guide intellectuals in a geometrical appreciation of abstraction: "it's still a question of knowing whether a given algebraic matrix is translatable in a spatial manner."[14] This spatial appreciation sometimes brought him back, perhaps a little too neatly, to Roman Jakobson, the linguist who theorized about the horizontal and vertical axes of poetic expression. For example, Lévi-Strauss once told Raymond Bellour and Catherine Clément that "reciprocal transformations are generated by a symmetry and inversion such that myths mutually reflect one another along such and such an axis."[15] The grid constructed from the intersection of axes provided the schematics for many of the diagrams accompanying his studies and attributable to his "mathematical" talent. More precisely, his vision was a geometrical one that was able to portray spatial relationships not obvious to the naked eye.

This talent for describing subtle spatial relationships has contributed to the developing role ascribed to the scientific mind during the twentieth century. Although he prefers to be known as "the scientist I try to be,"[16] he does not take all the credit for the scientific ties of ethnology. He liberally credits his scientific predecessors as the anthropologists Boas, Kroeber, Lowie, and Mauss, as well as the linguist Jakobson, the psychiatrist Freud, and the naturalist Jean-Jacques Rousseau. Nevertheless, Lévi-Strauss was so concerned with the world of underlying substance that his scientific posture created a problem popularly disguised as the fear of technology in humanists and artists. Appropriately, Robert Pirsig discussed the dual realities ensuing from this fear, two differing and irreconcilable dimensions: the romantic view of appearances held by artists and the classical vision of underlying scientific explanation.[17] Basically, the romantic view accounts for the fear of technology by many people in the twentieth century who appear to be overwhelmed by the demands for analysis and the threats of integrating humanity and machinery. As a result, this perspective entails the acceptance of a superficial view of reality without probing into the depths of a technological substratum. On the other hand, the scientific community has encouraged the understanding of underlying systems in order to reveal the networking of humans and machines. This split in dimensions, in ways of looking at reality, is fostered by the research conducted by Lévi-Strauss and is traceable to his inspiration by linguistics about the nature of the sign in human communication.

Signing Off

During his sojourn at the New School for Social Research in New York, Lévi-Strauss became acquainted with the leading linguists from the Prague School of structural linguistics. His methodological ties with Trubetskoy have already been cited. More important, the French ethnologist learned an appreciation of the nature of the sign in communication from Jakobson. A whole new world opened up for Lévi-Strauss. He appreciated the works of Ferdinand de Saussure, Emile Benveniste, and Jakobson himself such that the linguistic sign became understood for its properties as being arbitrarily assigned a given meaning, as being composed of referent and signifier, as being a basic human system of exchange.

But Lévi-Strauss would be no mere linguist. He extended the study of the linguistic sign into the ethnological milieu where the sign could be understood for its semiotic value, that is, for its operation in global human communication within and across cultural systems. He understood from Charles Saunders Peirce, the American pioneer in semiotics, that the sign was "what replaces something for someone."[18] A person chooses to have one thing replace another thing. The nature of that replacement concerned Lévi-Strauss. He understood transformation operating at a basic human level of communication, the symbolic representation of meaning within society. Here was the heart of the human spirit that he would portray for the rest of the world in his special spatial manner. One of his readers said it well by observing that Lévi-Strauss gave us "in fact . . . different codes transmitting the same message."[19] That same message was propagated in many forms, but basically it was reiterated quite simply in La Potière jalouse as "meaning is nothing but establishing a relationship among terms."[20]

The act of replacement, endemic to the sign, has a specific role in the research performed by Lévi-Strauss. As I have discussed, the incest taboo was revealed as a superficial manifestation of the exchange of women through kinship systems. Thus, appearances become replacements for an underlying act much more expansive than its surrogate. Similarly, Lévi-Strauss portrayed totemism as a fiction imposed by a dominant culture on what it would like to call "primitive" means of expression. Culture thus replaces nature through prejudicial communication on the part of an insensitive, subjugating group of people. As with signs, the replacement obliterates the referent so that an independent existence is given to the signifier. This insight into cultural exchange systems led Lévi-Strauss into a lifelong campaign on behalf of intercultural tolerance, and patience in the face of human differences.

The sign has enabled "civilized" peoples to obliterate differences with such linguistic formulas as primitive/civilized, nature/culture, and space/time. Cultural diversity enables us to appreciate the arbitrary nature of these formulas. Lévi-Strauss understood entropy and disorder to be two phenomena that have been transformed and disregarded by dominant cultures. He revealed that the identification of order with civilization precluded understanding the universal nature of humanity by preferring assimilation through transformation into known values.[21] Through his spatial translations of the myths, he sought to demonstrate an appreciation of differentiation through an expression of the system innate to a given mode of expression. And yet he, too, was subject to the same limitations inherent in the sign: it is an arbitrary replacement for the referent.

Lévi-Strauss identified certain patterns being repeated in cultures having no apparent relationships. For example, from his studies of myths in North American Indian tribes, he generalized that "myths are always reducible to other myths by similar transformations."[22] Of course, he applied the universal model of semiotic replacement— that is, that a sign replaces one thing for another—to myths in general. But he was so dogmatic in his presentations of these reductionist models that the arbitrariness of his own formulations of the patterns appeared lost in the fixed portrayals of his diagrams. We should recall that his formulation of "structure" was based on his view of the pervasiveness of change, in imitation of the natural permutations of the sign in human communication: "we must . . . recognize the primacy of change and consider structure as the way the observer translates an instantaneous [also photographic, like a snapshot] and artificial apprehension of a moving reality."[23] And

thus the "structure" was useful for studying transformations despite
its apparently contradictory nature as a fixed construct outside of
time.

And what about the role of progress in "civilization" as transformations and structures are juxtaposed from temporally and spatially isolated peoples? Lévi-Strauss assumed a unity in the human
spirit so he did not observe any progress within human consciousness. Instead, the permutations and transformations revealed by the
common human structures revealed new differences in attitudes to
which the human spirit could apply its "unchangeable abilities."[24]
As he considered the classic distinction between nature and culture,
Lévi-Strauss offered to the study of history what Greimas has called
"a better understanding of the models of transformation which historians likewise need."[25] As historians trace the effects of time on
human behavior, the studies by Lévi-Strauss on transformation are
especially pertinent. But in order to appreciate the dynamism and
spatio-temporal nature of meaning, history can be better appreciated
through the interwoven structures and transformations entailed in
his recasting of nature and culture.

Chapter Six

Can Nature Be Reintegrated into Culture?

Reviving the Debate of Nature versus Culture

Claude Lévi-Strauss addressed the question of progress in what is commonly known as our "civilization." He unearthed the eighteenth-century version of the answer clothed in the terms *nature* and *culture*. Since he admired Jean-Jacques Rousseau as one of his intellectual predecessors, the thorny issue was raised within the context of the solitary peripatetic's preference for "nature" and the "noble savage." The opposition of "natural things," so sympathetic to the human condition, to the urban jungle with its condescending cultural overtones generated spirited discussion subsequent to the "Quarrel of the Ancients and the Moderns" in eighteenth-century France. Likewise, *Tristes tropiques* (1955) appeared in an era wherein post–World War II technology complete with the atomic bomb set the scene for an appreciation of ethnological studies, particularly in the field of cultural anthropology. Lévi-Strauss would even make Rousseau a "patron saint" for these studies by pointing out that "in almost modern terms, Rousseau poses the central problem of anthropology, namely the passage from nature to culture."[1] Of course, to state an issue as a "problem" does not make it one. We must now examine what he meant by this "passage" and whether he was setting up a straw man for the purposes of engaging others in a discussion of the propriety of ethnology as a "modern" science.

The first issue in the debate over nature and culture was whether the distinction itself has any meaning. Although Lévi-Strauss was very involved in discriminating between appearances and substance, he did state the obvious by invoking a popular assumption that "it's apparently the opposition between human and animal behavior which provides the most striking example of the antinomy between culture and nature."[2] The key-word here is *apparently* because once again he sought to probe the depths to discover that the substance did

not support the "antinomy." The distinctions themselves had to be defined because even the oppositions between human and animal behavior were not mutually exclusive.

In defining the two terms, Lévi-Strauss elected to isolate geographically the territory in which each had a stake. On the one hand, ethnography was the discipline that studied "nature" by revealing the innate qualities of groups of people. In a way, there is some self-defense here. Since he was not formally schooled in ethnology and was criticized for lacking extensive field experience, one can appreciate his reflection that "ethnography is one of the rare authentic vocations: we can discover it in itself without ever having been taught how to do it."[3] Note the concern with innateness and how ethnology not only observes the internal cohesion of a human group but also offers its own disciplinary cohesion as something that can be learned from the inside. Hence, "nature," for Lévi-Strauss, meant the innate qualities of a particular identity. And human nature was the internal consistency of humanity, not unlike his conception of the human spirit.

On the other hand, "culture" was the concern of sociology, in the opinion of Lévi-Strauss.[4] Hence, society intervened to create needs distinct from those innate ones inherited by human "nature." He observed that "the relation between man and his needs is mediated by culture and cannot be conceived of simply in terms of nature."[5] So he found the term *nature* wanting when humanity was observed in a social context. His first insight into this lack was obtained from studying the incest taboo. Despite a history of scholarship on the problem, no one had succeeded as he had in identifying the prohibition with the economics of exchanging women as gifts. This taboo was thus a manifestation, not of a natural need (that is, innate), but of another type of need. The other type had more to do with phenomena external to the human condition and entailing "a mediation between the relationships of humanity and the world."[6] Let us recall the working definition of semiotics from Greimas: the study of how humanity conceives, organizes, and humanizes its world. Culture does appear to provide the stuff for understanding the gist of this communication between people and their world, especially a "mediation" between the two.

Lévi-Strauss showed that the mediation was a dominating kind in its manifestation of superiority either by virtue of progress or of the cumulative power of history. He observed culture shunning the spontaneous behavior of nature in favor of conformity and restraint according to a socially accepted norm.[7] The end-result of this process is that those groups of people "discovered" by ethnologists or cultural anthropologists outside the realm of accepted civilization are viewed as inferior or less developed. Rousseau's "noble savage" even inverted the order by implying a lack of nobility in civilization after the dominant order assimilated what was in the realm of nature.

A Question of Order

Lévi-Strauss would have us reexamine the nature/culture controversy in terms of his proposal for the universal human spirit as he revealed it operating in myths. Since he set out to show "how myths are coined in humanity without its conscious involvement,"[8] he would juxtapose myths as if the coincidence of similar stories precluded temporal and geographical disparities. By effectively dissolving these incongruities, he placed myths in a logical order wherein the distinctions of nature and culture assumed positions on the same plane of comprehension. The hierarchy, subsuming one to the other, imposed from the outside by the representatives of "culture," was revealed as false. Lévi-Strauss led some to believe that the apparently bogus issue was not so phony because, as one of his critics philosophized for him: "distinguishing nature and culture is useful in a good logical scheme, but it's difficult, and even impossible to discover a distinction that neat in concrete human experience."[9]

If it is not so neat, then what is the value of distinguishing between nature and culture within a logical scheme? Their positioning in the human spirit set the parameters for the work of Lévi-Strauss. On the one hand, his concern with nature was delineated in *La Pensée sauvage*. In contradistinction to August Comte's study of "primitive thought" ("la pensée sauvage"), Lévi-Strauss directed his concern with "primitive" peoples toward the goal of identifying "thought in its primitive state" ("la pensée à l'état sauvage"). By doing so, he could create a case for the universality of the human mind, despite the condescension of "cultured" societies toward the "primitive" groups assumed to be closer to nature. On the other hand, culture also concerns the identity of a given people. "Civilized thought" ("la pensée cultivée") reflected the influence of certain dominant ideologies regarding the gist of culture and civilization. Lévi-Strauss sought to find out what distinction "civilized thought" made for the human/animal differences: "what makes a human being really different from an animal is that, within humanity, a family could not exist if there were no society."[10] Hence, the human need for social identity accounts for the power in culture to include some groups and exclude others through the logical pattern of preferred modes of behavior.

However, Lévi-Strauss was intent upon demonstrating that "civilization" or those societies controlling the identity of "culture" had falsely viewed chronological "progress" such that "primitive" societies were assigned to a prelogical state. It was inappropriate to identify the groups of people outside or other than the dominant logical scheme as either "primitive" or prelogical, especially when the modes of thinking used by the estranged peoples were unknown to the dominant observers. While transposing the debate of nature versus culture into the logical arena, he also shifted the criteria from the chronological parameters of "progress" to the innate attributes of human logic revealed through storytelling. Instead of recognizing the ideological and historical ties between culture and nature, Lévi-Strauss understood these two to be so dissimilar as to constitute the geographical poles for "the cosmic dichotomy."[11]

This "cosmic dichotomy" referred to the universal presence of the human spirit. In his response to Jean-Paul Sartre's critique of the oversimplified analytical method of ethnography, Lévi-Strauss pointed to how "the savage mind totalizes"[12] rather than limiting itself to a particular logic, such as Sartre's "dialectical" model. This observation led the French ethnologist to claim that the "primitive" peoples offer microcosmic models for all humanity in the logic of their myths. Of course, this intellectual claim must be tempered by the critique that Lévi-Strauss was never able to converse easily with the native informants in their own language.[13] His knowledge of their logic was derived from studies carried out at a distance from "the state of nature."

In Search of Consistency

During his career, Lévi-Strauss did attenuate the role of the distinction between nature and culture for ethnography. He first revived the debate in 1949 in *Les Structures elémentaires de la parenté*. But by 1961 he had already reduced the distinction so that it was of "primarily methodological importance."[14] Accused of presupposing the universality of the human spirit, Lévi-Strauss sought to substitute a methodological consistency for an amalgamation of pre-suppositions. He found a way to respond to Sartre's promotion of the historically based "dialectical" method with the ethnologically accountable thesis of a "totalizing savage mind." This "totalizing" power helped Lévi-Strauss in discussing the "cosmic dichotomy" upon which the distinction nature/culture was modeled and which also set up the parameters for his discussions of the internal logic(s) of myths. A case in point is his concluding comparison of the Ge and Tupi stories in contradistinction to the Bororo tribal myths of Brazil: "The Ge thus make a natural category out of the raw/cooked matrix whereas the Tupi make a cultural category of the raw/cooked matrix."[15]

But what did Lévi-Strauss mean by using "natural" and "cultural" as logical predicates? An architectural model of human logic was constructed by this self-proclaimed "handyman" ("bricoleur") in the workshop of ethnology. Since "natural" had the implication of "in-nate" for Lévi-Strauss, he sought to discover the minimal framework for human logic in the stories narrated by isolated societies. The "cultural" component then was an elaboration of the intellectual networks found in "primitive" myths. Lévi-Strauss was the one to provide the blueprints for these buildings of human logic. The integrity of the buildings was to be reproduced by him as he resolved the duplicity of subject and object so crucial to phenomenology and to the "human sciences" in their claim for objective analysis. The "primitive" societies were viewed as "other," as objects separate from the subjectivity of the investigators from dominant cultures. But through the pervasive plan or blueprint, popularly called the "structure" by Lévi-Strauss, he united this dichotomous universe within the overall rubric of the human spirit. This architectural analogy also recalls Martin Heidegger's postulate of language as the "House of Being"[16] in the sense that methodological concepts of thinking are formed by how we choose to communicate. Lévi-Strauss examined the components of this "House" and studied how they were assembled from common human parameters for communication.

Methodologically, Lévi-Strauss thus addressed the origins and the future fate of humanity. With myths as the immediate media by which to examine these concerns among cultured and primitive societies, he explored the universal plan behind the storytelling skills so apparently different and yet substantially similar in their logical framework. He would have us understand the Oedipus myth, for example, as a story that superficially challenges the incest taboo. But once again the obvious was too simple for him. Since he had revealed that the incest taboo was an example of the cultural dominance of women, he applied that insight to the story of Oedipus by explaining this myth as "the denial of the autochthonous origins of man."[17] *Autochthonous* means "born of the earth," not unlike *natural* as opposed to *cultural*. While the Oedipus myth was a rejection of the indigenous self-sufficiency of humanity, the story likewise affirmed our cultural origins and continual return to these disguised ties in an apparently natural reversion. So it is with the incest taboo, at least according to *Les Structures elémentaires de la parenté*. Oedipus thus became the incarnation of a basic principle linking all myths: that humanity reiterates its cultural origins through its mythmaking and storytelling talents. I will return to this idea in chapter 9 to discuss how myths "think" despite humanity's conscious aims for their meanings. For this discussion of nature and culture, the Oedipus myth, as analyzed by Lévi-Strauss, reminds us that culture is also a principle innate to the ways humanity thinks about itself collectively. So innateness is a common denominator for both nature and culture in the Lévi-Strauss scheme of things.

Investing in "Homo Faber"

Lévi-Strauss's "method" is often identified with a handyman's art ("le bricolage"). This association brings together the innate skills of "doing it yourself" with a learned consistency. Lévi-Strauss thus encouraged a rethinking of the contrast between nature and culture such that the distinction should be revealed as a specious one, having no validity by which peoples distinguish themselves as superior to one another. Indeed, the historian Hayden White has shown that the "noble savage" idea arising from ascribing certain peoples to the arena of "nature" does become a fetish that leads to race and class warfare.[18] And Lévi-Strauss decidedly addressed the problem with his essays *Race et histoire* (1952, 1971, 1983) whereby he pointed out that both ethnocentrism and xenophobia are dangers resulting from facile applications of the nature/culture distinctions. Instead, he encouraged people to understand humanity as innately possessing both natural and cultural dimensions, as exemplified by the little appreciated methods of the handyman.

As he applied the method of combining nature and culture into a single vision, Lévi-Strauss sometimes found other examples of the "dramatic encounter"[19] between the distinctions among various peoples. He himself was not without fault, however, in being caught up in the very stereotypic view of "progress" assumed by the domination of culture over nature. For example, in 1966, he compared two of his "mythologiques" thus: "The mythology of the cooking unfolds in the correct way ['le bon sens'] . . . from nature to culture, whereas the mythology of honey goes against the current by regressing from culture to nature."[20] He would later realize that he, too, was subject to a facile view of culture (note his vocabulary pointing to the "progress" and "correct way" of moving from natural to cultural identity and the "regressive" association with moving away from the cultural).

In all of the peoples and myths he analyzed, he was able to identify marriage acting as "a mediating mechanism between a nature and a culture initially understood to be disjointed."[21] And indeed, if we were to understand the distinctions of nature/culture as functionally equivalent to the separation of the natural and human laws or heredity and tradition, then human mating and its social sanction do come together in a rite of passage into socially acceptable behavior which is also innately inspired. The incest taboo regulates the choices and commerce of the mediating mechanism known as marriage. The mediation, however, is a compromise in which the socially accepted norms are superimposed on natural behavior in order to receive social sanction. Hence, the individual is subsumed by the group such that "homo faber," the human tool-maker—commonly accepted as a symbol of acculturation—negotiates an innate integrity for a functional role among others.

Lévi-Strauss differed from Jean-Jacques Rousseau regarding the influence of nature/culture on the division of labor in societies. Rousseau's essay on the inequality of man had clearly associated the division of labor between man and woman as natural and innate to the sexes. By contrast, Lévi-Strauss observed that once marriage imposed its cultural sanctions on individuals, then family and the divisions of labor ensued from cultural domination.[22] This is a logical construct, not one of domination and/or subjugation, because the relationship between humanity and its needs becomes more complex as other people enter into an individual's life. Nature is understood here to be inadequate, as Lévi-Strauss's study of totemism demonstrated.[23]

Despite promoting the view that nature and culture are not mutually exclusive terms, he realized that this idea was not universally accepted. He was not only raising a straw man, but also addressing pressing issues for our times, namely racism, xenophobia, and hegemonic imperialism. He put the challenge point-blank to the natural sciences to reintegrate culture into nature and to lead the way to a nonprogressive manner of understanding history.[24]

Chapter Seven

What Happens to History?

Time without Progress

Claude Lévi-Strauss did not completely preclude the role of history from his "structuralist" views of humanity. It has often been noted that, because he insisted that "societies don't have any history,"[1] his weltanschauung was not compatible with history. However, the problem is not that simple. Granted that Lévi-Strauss qualified the relationship between ethnography and history such that history was not the final arbiter in professional debates. He was especially uncomfortable with the ideological domination of Western civilization and its concomitant investments in the necessity of "Progress." He would not buy into either of these tenets.

Instead, Lévi-Strauss would consistently demonstrate the disparity inherent in the French word for "history": *histoire* means both "story" and "history." His ethnographical examination of myths made the case that one's history is a narrated event with value-systems, such as progress, built into the very arrangement of the story. The "structuralist" form of ethnography also revealed the possibility for a very different type of history, one not dependent on defining "progress" nor "origins" in its storytelling activity. Although many of the myths analyzed by Lévi-Strauss were stories accounting for the development or evolution of certain tribal or group practices, the collective body of these myths did not show a common justification for the existence of "progress" or "an origin." This is significant for Lévi-Strauss because his research was not only intent upon finding the human spirit uniting all peoples together but also upon demonstrating that Western civilization did not have the final say on what was the nature of history. The history of Western civilization had imposed too great a hegemony upon how the human spirit expressed itself. Lévi-Strauss proposed to free us from the domination of this version of "history" by exposing how other cultures conceived of themselves and their histories through their stories.

He offered another model of how history could operate. Instead of a "progress" that is necessary and continuous throughout Western history, Lévi-Strauss discovered that progress "proceeds by leaps and bounds, or as the biologists would say, by mutations."[2] The biological model allowed him to acknowledge diversity in time and space for heterogeneous societies so that all need not be judged by the same spatio-temporal criteria. In this way, a society could express its own self-identity without the pejorative association of either inferiority or subordination to another group. By contrast, history, as it had been practiced in Western societies, "was a category interior to certain societies, a way in which hierarchical societies conceive of themselves rather than a milieu . . . for all human groups."[3] Lévi-Strauss was willing to let those practitioners of Western history continue with their concerns.[4] But he would not allow this history a false reign over ethnography. He wanted to separate the two disciplines because, as opposed to history, with its dominant ideologies abetting unilateral views and the concomitant problems of racism and political hegemony, ethnography could reveal that "the forms of life and thought that transcend History constitute a permanent hope for mankind."[5]

A Question of Method

In distinguishing ethnography from history, Lévi-Strauss was intent upon establishing the methodological integrity of the discipline he had adopted without any formal training. His concern with method was generated by his heated debate with Jean-Paul Sartre about the importance of history. Lévi-Strauss was quick to react to Sartre's insistence upon the promise of totality given by historical dialectics by filling the last chapter of La Pensée sauvage with such quips as: "History is only a method to which no specific object corresponds"; and "In Sartre's system, History plays the role of a myth."[6] Much of their debate must be appreciated as another example of fashionable, Parisian intellectual gamesmanship. Sartre had contrasted the "systems" identified in the ethnography of Lévi-Strauss with his own historical "totality." Nevertheless, in one of the passages cited above, Lévi-Strauss, with considerable irony, spoke of Sartre's "system" in its "mythical" construct of history. Their debate did not resolve any issues, but did serve to highlight Lévi-Strauss as an advocate of "structuralism" in opposition to the venerated role of history. Their overly intellectual fireworks did not generate much substance so they will not concern us here (Lionel Abel has given us a good overview of their arguments if you are interested in the specifics).[7]

Lévi-Strauss did not so much negate the role of history as he did qualify its authoritative presence. Indeed, he insisted that "the ethnologist respects history, but he does not assign it a privileged value."[8] This "privileged value" of history was alluded to again when he acclaimed the work of Raymond Aron, "an intellectual and a philosopher who never agreed to make History into a privileged place where humanity would be assured of being able to find its truth."[9] The "truth" of humanity lies in the human spirit if Lévi-Strauss were to tell us about it. And history is merely a methodological apparatus to guide us, at times, toward "truth." There is no repository of truth within Sartre's "dialectical totality" of history. Lévi-Strauss had once espoused Marxism, so he knew the dialectical method. But he preferred analytical skills to allow him to understand the "structure" or "system" of the "human spirit." History and the dialectical method gave him contextual parameters for the subject matter of humanity; but his focus shifted with ethnology away from a Marxist view and toward an innate, almost biological, perspective of cross-cultural mutations in human thinking.

An Un-Marxian History

Indeed, Lévi-Strauss has been accused of being un-Marxian (rather than anti-Marxist) in his presentation of "historicity" within his "structuralist" agenda. Critics such as George Steiner and Henri Lefebvre[10] have noted that he was too naive in his rejection of the importance of the dialectical role of history in ethnological study. And yet Lévi-Strauss did not completely throw out history in his work with myths and other anthropological phenomena. He did state that "only historical development permits weighing and evaluating the components of the present in their respective relationships."[11] Of course, he did not have a positivistic temperament to validate events and the materialistic contexts of human society. Instead, his historical sense led to the verification of patterns then universalized by him into mathematical formulas and equations.

This tendency to universalize specific phenomena has been called a "geological" time-sense by the British anthropologist Edmund Leach[12] in apparent deference to Lévi-Strauss's identification of geology as one of his three intellectual mistresses (along with Marxism and psychoanalysis). The implication of temporal layers from geology amplifies Lévi-Strauss's obsession with distinguishing appearance from substance. With this insight, we can appreciate his work as creating profiles of the human spirit by uncovering successive layers of human thought from different epochs without depending upon chronological or dialectical order to predetermine his resulting model.

The "structuralist" profile given to us by Lévi-Strauss is not one that accounts for evolution, development, or progress. Part of the reason for this is that he believed that the human spirit is universal and timeless. For that reason, he understood his task as an ethnographer to be outside of time. He portrayed the ethnographer as being "condemned to static study: History is what he misses the most."[13] Professionally and intellectually, he had to relegate history to the role of a handmaiden of ethnology: it can help us "to give a wider meaning to civilization itself."[14] Sartre's reply in 1968 was that, with this perspective, "history appears as a purely passive phenomenon."[15] And indeed history was passive for Lévi-Strauss because it was no science in itself. It offered a methodology of dealing with time; but history presumed origins, continuity, progress, development, temporal consistency, and linear modeling: all of which constricted the analytical ethnologist too much. And so Lévi-Strauss sought a method to enable him to appreciate the mutations of the human spirit without necessarily acknowledging the presumptions of history as to the ultimate outcome of his analyses.

The models of biology and geology gave Lévi-Strauss the scientific inspiration he sought for ethnology. He believed that "all that was truly creative, all that shook up our ideas about humanity and our ways of thinking, came from science."[16] So the models of mutations in biology and layers of sediment in geology led him to look into a historical accounts of the role of time within the human spirit. His research into myths was especially revealing in that he began to realize, with his study of myths, that time was an order invented to account for the succession of change and similarity in the identity of a people. This "order" was internal to the myths narrated by such a people. Thus, "time" was found to have its own logic, layered within the suspenseful concatenation of events and characters in the stories people tell about their origins and destinies. Lévi-Strauss described this layering as "the order continuously [depuis toujours] dreamed by the myths themselves."[17] The "time" of a given myth was not manifest, but "dreamed," nonconsciously layered within the narrative. Of course, the concept of nonconscious, which I shall discuss more fully in chapter 9, is another manifestation of his mistrust of the obvious and his consequent exploration of the latent possibilities beyond the surface of human behavior. Within the context of his geological motivation for the study of time, however, the dream provided Lévi-Strauss with the potential for analysis and for a "vertical structure" to a story which appears to be narrating a certain "horizontal" plot structure. But the myths themselves convey an order independent from the message intended by the narrator in stringing together the elements of a suspenseful tale.

The "vertical order" in myths was usually not similar from one myth to another, and yet it corresponded to an awareness by Lévi-Strauss of the mutational character of all myths from the human spirit. Although many of his critics have pointed to the lack of unity among his many reductive formulas analyzing the artifacts from peoples throughout the world, and complained about the inconclusive nature of the evidence concerning the existence of a universal human spirit, Lévi-Strauss continued to maintain its role in the temporal development of groups examined by ethnologists: "existing societies are the result of great transformations which occurred unexpectedly in the human spirit; . . . an uninterrupted chain of real events links those facts to those we can observe."[18] Notice his use of "occurred unexpectedly" in order to include the nonconscious element into the generation of the "mutations" leading up to the constitution of social groups. In addition, Lévi-Strauss allowed for the existence of empirically based history within his scheme of things with the postulate of "an uninterrupted chain of real events." However, the notion of "mutants," that is, spinoffs in the strict evolution of a species, provided him with a model by which to critique the chronological pattern of history and to replace it with his "structuralist history," one that promised to be more "scientific" than the dialectical form demanded by Sartre.

Lévi-Strauss learned that social forms and communication could be studied scientifically in ethnology. Hence, he advocated the understanding of a "history" that could be sensitive to the various orders of time found in differing cultures. Despite the cry from his opponents who could not understand how "structuralism" could be reconciled with history, it was a very sober Lévi-Strauss who chal-

lenged that "it is History therefore, combining forces with sociology
and semiotics, which must allow the analyst to break the circle of
a non-temporal confrontation. . . ."[19] The arguments of his semiotic prolegomenon for sociology will be discussed in chapter 10.
Suffice it to say for now that he challenged the naive repudiation
of "structuralism" by the defenders of Western history.

Responding to that challenge, he had already laid the groundwork
for his "structuralist history" whereby time and structures were
integrated into cohesive analyses of human behavior. In his inaugural
lecture at the Collège de France (1960), he had referred to the
components of "structuralist history," which shouldn't shock historians, in his opinion, because "some facts depend on a static and
irreversible time, and others on a mechanical and reversible time."[20]
His portrayal of "history" thus entailed views of time as contin-
gencies, pluridimensional and dependent upon the focus of analysis.
Indeed, he was aware that empirical events were crucial in the way
one accounted for the role of time in scientific investigation.

Historical Structuralism

Nonetheless, as opposed to horizontal or chronological presentations of events, Claude Lévi-Strauss preferred a vertical or stratigraphical account of events. Inspired by a geological model with
the insight that historical events help to explain the intellectual
layers or weltanschauung of the stories or myths invested with belief
by successive generations of a people, he often ignored the events
themselves because he was more concerned about getting to the core
of the myths, to the human spirit generating the structure of the
stories, rather than with the process by which the stories were
encoded into various mutations. Hence, he could say that "structural
analysis therefore doesn't take exception to history . . . and con-
cedes to it a place in the first order of things . . . by acknowledging
the power and the lifelessness of the event."[21] The "power" of
history's layering effect on myths and other cultural artifacts is
quickly contrasted with its nonvitality in his project of isolating
the intellectual core of humanity.

The "power" of the historical event in the "first order of things"
does give history an important role in the structuralist method of
Lévi-Strauss. His hermeneutic opponent, Paul Ricoeur, observed
two poles of time operating within the structuralist enterprise. Ri-

coeur called them the totemic and the kerygmatic.[22] These two extremes can help us to appreciate the geologically inspired stratigraphic view of time in the work of Lévi-Strauss. On the one hand, the kerygmatic or hermeneutic conception of time was a view of time as the initial, rich investment of meaning followed by continuous reinvestments of meaning. This is not so very far from the historical event, as Lévi-Strauss viewed it. On the other hand, the totemic or structuralist presentation of time was quite distinct in that continuity was "shattered" or "broken" by the analytical enterprise of forging a formula in which all the temporal strata were reduced. At times, Lévi-Strauss appeared to realize the temporal extremes within his domain. The scientific method could not account for all variances in his subject matter. He acknowledged the role of incertitude in the human sciences and went so far as to admit that "without forgetting that a historian can sometimes work as an ethnologist and an ethnologist as a historian, . . . even the social sciences have their uncertain relationships."[23] For Lévi-Strauss, neither history nor ethnology can exclude the other from its domain. Structuralism and history were not so mutually exclusive as they had first appeared to be.

In order to justify the intertwining roles of history and ethnology, Lévi-Strauss returned to Marx, whose writings advocated an internal coherence in addressing society's problems. Rather than the Marxian dialectical materialism, however, Lévi-Strauss retrieved a sense of history that haunted him throughout his work. He was fond of citing Marx's comment that "humanity makes its own history, but it is not aware of doing so."[24] History is thus a myth entailing nonconscious conceptions of time. It also involved Lévi-Strauss himself in its telling since in *Tristes tropiques* he had admitted that "anthropology affords me intellectual satisfaction: as a form of history, linking up at opposite ends with world history and my own history, it thus reveals the rationale common to both."[25] His "intellectual satisfaction" with anthropology as a "form of history" waned as he sought a scientific method to explore the innate character of human nature without predispositions such as those of coherence or chronology found in philosophy and history. Instead, he analyzed time itself as offering intellectual interest as order "dreamed" or coined by the innate structure of a myth. The quality of the order as "dreamed" leads us to continue our discussion of the work of Lévi-Strauss in the area of the symbol and the nonconscious, two components of his own weltanschauung that not only led him to remake history but also to direct it toward his goal of revealing the human spirit.

Chapter Eight
Symbolic Representation

Beyond Appearances

Claude Lévi-Strauss was long concerned with what went beyond appearances. His ethnological research led him to accommodate that concern somewhat when he realized the presence of symbols functioning within cultural artifacts. The symbol, a sign representing a deeper or wider meaning than it possesses in itself, provided Lévi-Strauss with an argument for bonding surface and substance into a coherence ignored heretofore in favor of linguistic disjunction, an arbitrary assignment of meaning at the core of representation itself. He did not deny the semiotic disjunction of symbols but instead demonstrated how different cultures "throw together" (*symballein* means to throw together, to compare) heterogeneous symbolic values in the same sign. Similar to the effect of synecdoche (commonly known as metonymy), by which a part is accepted for its whole, the symbol is more than the appearance of a sign in that it leads to a whole system of culturally conditioned values and ideologies.

The symbol thus became a key to unlocking the linguistic model of the sign linking surface and substance in society for Lévi-Strauss. His prior pejorative understanding of surface as deceptive or unimportant to his pursuit of the human spirit was reoriented by viewing the symbol (*symbolon* means a token, a pledge, and a sign by which one infers something else) as connection between the individual and a universal code linking humanity together. The symbol effectively bridged his immediate ethnological subjects such as myths, taboos, masks, and totems with the mathematical formulas he produced to outline the universal features of the human spirit. The symbol linked these realms and promised to provide a map of that human core he sought to define and which constantly seemed to evade him.

The Power in the Mask

Lévi-Strauss studied the symbolic value of ceremonial masks among peoples in remote areas of South America. The masks revealed the power of hiding and the capability of appearances to retain power and strength even though levels of reality were expounded by the very use of these disguises. Among the Caduveo in Brazil, for example, he discovered that ceremonial masks were part of a system of "hieroglyphics describing an inaccessible golden age."[1] Hence, their masks were ever-present reminders (signs) of the tribal ties to the past, of the cultural heritage being acted out with the masks, and of their bonds to mysteries and to the occult.

In themselves, the masks are simple signs representing super-natural associations, and also serve as part of a network of values linking quotidian concerns with universal attributes of lasting significance to a given people. This need for permanence was translated into myths whose "goal [was] to explain the legendary or super-natural origin [of the mask(s)] and to anchor their role in ritual, economy, and society. . . ."[2] As symbols of other systems of values, the masks obtain power through their link between appearance and substance as exemplified by the observation by Lévi-Strauss that, once women use the mask or possess it, they concomitantly gain access to exogamous marriage.[3]

The symbolic value of the mask thus provided a very real acces-sibility from quotidian, provincial concerns to an exoticism prom-ising entry into another value-system. Literally, the mask belonged to a ritualistic order as a ceremonial sign. Possession of the mask had a talismanic effect because, as Lévi-Strauss remarked, "every-thing comes easily to the possessor of the mask."[4] The magical aura of the mask contributed to the symbolic transformation of objects contiguously associated with the mask on the level of the sign. For example, empty seashells on masks attained a "mystical"[5] value by comparison with leather, identified primarily by its feral origins. Likewise, certain metals, such as copper and bronze, had a symbolic status on the masks and became talismans by their entry into the supernatural network associated with the ceremonial masks. This "network" was not so much what the masks literally represented because they often did not simply portray a certain deity or demon, but rather they are transformations of the quotidian order through the combination of "mystical" components and objects not representing anything at all. The nonrepresentational portion of the masks pointed toward the "other," nonquotidian order in which the masks functioned as symbols, or conveyors of difference.

This different order opened up by the symbolic functioning of the ceremonial masks was a network or system of relationships among the values held by a given society. Ideally, Lévi-Strauss would have liked to discover links among these networks through the storytelling activity in which the symbols were initially placed as signs with privileged positions in the context of a story invested with belief by a people and thus adopted as a myth. His studies of kinship indeed revealed subtle networks in our culturally conditioned taboos about appropriate marriage partners and directed us to look for types of exchange and economy that are more widespread (for example, the male trading of women by controlling the choice in marriage partnerships) than they may appear to be once couched in social disguises (the incest taboo).

Lévi-Strauss thus would have us believe that symbolic fields accede to a human intellectual matrix in which value systems have a certain universal common denominator. Lévi-Strauss never provided the proof that this was so, yet he intimated that even kinship patterns were part of the human spirit and were models for its manifestation in that they, too, were "systems of symbols."[6] Since Lévi-Strauss demonstrated that human thought tends to express itself in anecdotal (narrative) fashion, then the story told by kinship systems is an example of how the human mind weaves its symbols according to patterns and systems discoverable to those who go beyond the geometric appearances to find the algebra subtending the linear connections.

The mathematical operators in his discussion of ethnological problems tell us about how Lévi-Strauss related his scientific or positivistic method to symbols. Mathematics gave him the instruments, by means of its formulas, to separate the elements of a myth and then to reassemble them into a coherent deduction, an approximation of human meaning in an anthropological artifact. He was keenly aware of the role of the symbol in directing his method because ". . . an attentive and meticulous observation totally concentrated on the concrete concomitantly discovers its principle and its outcome in symbolism."[7] Since symbols are links between the sense-perceived realm of signs and the intellectual domain of the human spirit, which Lévi-Strauss was intent upon revealing, the mathematical terms and schematics he used allowed him to move along the continuum between the two realms. Although he noted that "meaning is not directly perceived but deduced,"[8] it must be noted that he did postulate the existence of the intellectual pole for the symbol: that elusive property he called the human spirit. During much of his ethnographic studies, he moved back and forth between the two poles of symbols rather than merely from the concrete to the abstract, or from the specific sign to the network of meaning to which the symbol gave him access.

External Analogies

A symbol for Claude Lévi-Strauss did not "mean" *in itself* but always referred to something other or foreign to itself. As the medium of exchange between the concrete and the abstract, the symbol played a crucial role in relating the semiotic appearances of an ethnological artifact to its relationship as part of the "structure" of a much larger ensemble, a product of the human spirit. So if a symbol was coherent, it obtained this cohesion from ties external to itself but within various systems (for example, kinship, myth, totemism). Therein, the symbol cemented the components of the systems by directing their relationship through its function as the conduit of meaning.

Examples of this coherence abound in the *Mythologiques* wherein he developed symbols crucial to establishing the patterns of myths. The Botocudo myths of eastern Brazil provided a specific instance whereby the analogous symbols of honey and tobacco pointed toward the limits in the power of the people to control their own fate.[9] On the one hand, raw honey and diluted honey represented nature and culture interacting within the tribal storytelling customs to exemplify the ties of the tribe with nature and also to express their need to make their mark by diluting its raw power. On the other hand, the smoke produced by mixing red pepper with fire was a ritualized ceremony by which the tribe acted out its need to transform nature from a passive adornment (tobacco) into an active manifestation of its powerlessness (prayer to a deity). The symbols thus acted as components in a system of values translated from other realms and yet remaining as ties to an external reality.

This functional role of a symbol was also assigned by Lévi-Strauss in his several attempts at literary analysis. Although some literary analysts such as Michael Riffaterre would have preferred that the ethnologist not have invaded the realm of written poetry with linguistic and anthropological methods, nevertheless Lévi-Strauss did acknowledge the importance of literary communication by attempting to analyze the semiotics of some written poems. Two noteworthy examples are his presentation of "Les Chats" (by Baudelaire) with Roman Jakobson and an analysis of "Les Colchiques" (by Apollinaire). The symbols in these poems allowed Lévi-Strauss to demonstrate how the human spirit is writing and being written concomitantly. The symbol is the bridge between the active thinker using the sign of the "meadow saffron" (*colchique* in French) blowing in the wind to reflect upon the eyes and eyelids of the beloved and this same thinker being thought by the system of correspondences between the natural world of flowers and the language of lovers.[10] Lévi-Strauss was thus able to show that the symbol is functional in various modes of communication to link different registers of activity. There is no privilege to oral or written cultures regarding the efficacy of their stories in presenting the human spirit. The symbol is a universal feature sought by Lévi-Strauss in his pursuit of the key to exposing the universal human spirit.

His pursuit was allied with the scientific pretensions of analysis. Perhaps science promised him a rigorous identity with "truth" inspired by his early philosophical training at the Sorbonne. Nevertheless, the association of ethnology and science struck a raw nerve among some of his peers. Sartre's objections to the "dialectical" method were complemented by Ricoeur's complaints concerning what was not being said by Lévi-Strauss about the necessary relationship between the symbol and interpretation. Ricoeur's point was that a symbol only "means" within a structure at a specific moment in time so that ". . . structure represents a cross-section of rationality at a given moment. . . ."[11] within which a symbolic system functions. Hence, Lévi-Strauss was challenged to account for the role of interpretation at the specific moment of his intervention to explain the role of a symbolic system. Ricoeur's development of "hermeneutics" addressed the situation of symbolic activity in the realm of psychology, but Lévi-Strauss was to expand its understanding in the cultural and social realm.

The hermeneutic critique of Lévi-Strauss was not a simple one for him to redress. And it was also a necessary critique because it mandated that Lévi-Strauss take a closer look at his idea of the bond between the individual human being (Ricoeur's insight to the structure operating in "a given moment") and the universal human spirit which symbols verified for him. His reply was to create a Janus-like understanding of symbolism. For Lévi-Strauss, a symbol looked in opposite directions by linking the individual with humanity. He would have us understand a symbol as having dual activities, thus presenting "a neat symmetry" because the two symbolizing activities "reply to mental necessities of the same type, oriented either toward the body or to society and the world."[12]

The symbol is thus situated at the center of human communication for all cultures in that it uniquely regulates the "traffic" between systems of values and the personal meaning from an individual at a specific historical moment. Hence, the revised understanding given by Lévi-Strauss to history, structure, system, and binary operatives was fully realized in the position assigned to the symbol within human communication. His characterization of this position as providing "neat symmetry" may engender suspicious concerns about his need to impose order from the outside. However, his observation was inspired, as I shall discuss in chapter 9, by a sensitivity for the coherence of the human psyche from within its functional situation of symbolic activity.

His adaptation of a scientist's role within ethnology made some readers uneasy with his speculations about symbols. The rigorous mathematical logic of his analyses of myths and the positivistic rigor with which he collected data for his studies demonstrated the two extremes of his scientific method: the first, an abstract and tightly knit argumentation using a symbolic system for the initiated; the second, a reliance upon collecting facts and data verified by association with specific tribes in defined geographical milieus. The "uneasiness" of his readers comes with his discussion of symbols by relating his two activities. The abstract arena of the human spirit is quite distinct from the rituals of daily activities performed by peoples separated from one another by time and space. We can thus appreciate the confusion of a reader who notes that "one can't be certain whether, fantasy-like or fantastic, he [Lévi-Strauss] is really real or for real, or whether it really matters if he's wearing the cape of magic or the mantle of science."[13] The complexity of his writing style as well as the subject matter elicit this sort of reaction. An example is his study of witch doctors and the role of incantation in the symbolism of the believers. His insights may help us to understand his own possible impact on those who are affected by his spells: "The cure brings together contrasting poles, assures the passage from one to the other, and gives testimony to a total experience, the coherence of the psychic universe, itself the projection of the social universe."[14] Here we also have part of the source of our discomfort with Lévi-Strauss: he promised a cure to the fragmentation of humanity from its world. We are leery of promises about a holistic medicine for what ails us because Lévi-Strauss did not offer us an obvious solution. Not only did he view symbols as our forms of "external analogy," bonds between our intellectual and our physical needs; but he also pointed out that once disclosed, the symbolic system would reveal the pattern of our universal humanity. And indeed he pushed on with his program "to effect the passage from 'external analogy' to 'internal homology.' "[15]

An Internal Homology

The psychic coherences suggested by symbolic systems point to an internal network in which resides the human spirit so tautened by Lévi-Strauss. Of course, the social context of the symbols was much more obvious so he set out to establish the correspondences between the social and the intellectual. As he deciphered the social and cultural values attributed to symbols, he realized that an intellectual model lay beneath the surface of the signs so common as to have more than a role within the daily rituals of a given people. Early in his career (1955), he noted that "human societies, like individual human beings, never create absolutely: all they can do is to choose certain combinations from a repertory of ideas which it should be possible to reconstitute."[16] This "repertory of ideas" pointed toward a certain intellectual determinism common to societies and individuals. Lévi-Strauss hoped that the symbolic systems would give him access to the index of this repertory so he could reveal its contents to the world.

As we look at his work, we do not find this index. Instead, we note the conspicuous presence of formulas to link symbols to each other and to other elements of a massive plan or "structure" of the psychic and social systems. These formulas contain still other mathematical symbols inserted by Lévi-Strauss to represent symbolic relationships within the intellectual or psychic plane of activity. What he effectively gave us by these formulas were maps of intellectual ensembles he identified as being also social and/or cultural media for cohesion. He discovered that these taboos, myths, masks, and other cultural artifacts signified both for humanity in general and for a social entity in the specific. By identifying these maps of intellectual cohesion, he sought to exemplify the patterns for the "internal homology" of human thinking. Indeed, they are only patterns. But they are islands, territories surveyed and measured, which can be linked once their locations and dimensions are revealed.

Lévi-Strauss did advocate linking these patterns together. Almost twenty years after postulating the finite "repertory of ideas," he suggested that the intensive study of social systems by cultural anthropology should be done "profoundly enough . . . to elaborate a kind of universal code, capable of expressing the common properties of specific structures."[17] Note that profundity is the means for arriving at this "common" or universal model for humanity. By "profundity," Lévi-Strauss continuously meant a reality beneath the surface, something beyond appearances. And yet he did not succeed in discovering the "internal homology" for humanity. Instead, his research revealed that the determinism in human behavior was not an intellectual one. His study of linguistics and of Marcel Mauss's insights into gifts combined to remind Lévi-Strauss of the material reality of symbols and of the fact that the signifier precedes and determines the signified. Meaning is not contained within the symbol itself but is obtained by its position, its "ethnographic context,"[18] according to Lévi-Strauss. In his research he established the parameters of that context by indicating the social and cultural determinism of the symbol. Ultimately, he hoped to find the human spirit there in his account of creativity within symbolic activity, so uniquely human.

The Creative Differential

In his studies of the rituals of human behavior, Lévi-Strauss noticed that symbols were part of the human need to be distinguished from animals. Lévi-Strauss identified this need for differentiation in even the most rudimentary practices of human survival: "If men deny their real animal nature in deference to their humanity through alimentary taboos, it's because they need to assume symbolic characteristics . . . to create the differences. . . ."[19] Symbolic activity is thus an effect of human creativity in its search for self-definition, specifically expressing the uniqueness of what it is that makes us human. The symbols themselves isolate certain signs and give them a privileged position among other signs. Lévi-Strauss focused upon the privilege given to symbols by elaborating their systemic ties between their external analogies and the internal homology of thinking. The bilateral method of his analyses reflected insights into the creativity of the symbol because he would have symbols be generated by dichotomous tensions at the very core of human thought. In fact, he observed at one point that "the constraints characteristic to the functioning of human thought orient the formation of human symbols . . . and explain how they are opposed and articulated among each other."[20] Hence, not only is the functioning of the human mind reflected in symbolic activity but also the source of symbolic activity can be found therein.

The intellectual creativity that generates symbols often does not do so in an obvious fashion. Much of the research done by Lévi-Strauss was concerned with revealing the deep structures of this creativity reflected in symbols. Recall his insights into the incest taboo whereby women were converted into symbols of economic exchange. Indeed, he identified the phenomenon as fantasizing about the reality of women as persons and transforming them into things because of the need to express human distinctiveness with symbolic activity: "The emergence of symbolic thought necessitated that women, like speech, had to be things to be exchanged."[21] This perspective on the incest taboo revealed symbolic activity as a lever to examine semiosis, communicative behavior. Do symbols contain information to be given simply to others and exchanged in disguised forms such as taboos? Or did Lévi-Strauss point to symbolic activity as indicative of metamorphosis within the human spirit? Yes, he did advocate sensitivity for the impact of change and for the adjustments to it by involving itself in the transformational character of signs. He himself seemed to be in search of a reality that could survive change and somehow be immutable despite the political, racial, and generational differences that generated so much controversy in the world.

Symbols held the key to that reality for Lévi-Strauss. But it was Jacques Lacan, the psychoanalyst, who set symbols within the context of the unconscious and allowed Lévi-Strauss to explore the functioning of the symbolic as part of a triadic scaffolding of the mind. This triad involved the symbolic function in tension with the "real" and the "imaginary." So symbols only revealed a corner of the human spirit, but nevertheless Lévi-Strauss was embarking on an exciting exploration of the latent underpinnings of those privileged signs called symbols. The symbols themselves weren't the issue. They were manifestations of a hidden Being lurking somewhere in a nonconscious realm where he sought to find the links with the "real" and the "imaginary." The "real" was very similar to the "external analogies" of symbols. But interwoven in nonconscious activity is the role of the "imaginary," which had to be explained within the creative thrust of human thinking. So, with Lacan as his enlightened guide, he descended into the depths of non-conscious activity to explain why "the vocabulary used by myths refers back to the three orders of the real, the symbolic, and the imaginary."[22]

Chapter Nine

Nonconscious Functioning

Toward the Imaginary

Masks were very intriguing to Claude Lévi-Strauss. He understood them to be models of how humanity disguises its conscious aims. Something else also lurked on the other side of conscious designs. His early flirtations with a scientific spirit and the empirical method led him to believe that ethnology had to be rooted in phenomena, the part of human thinking that Jacques Lacan called "the real." As Lévi-Strauss worked more and more with symbols and came to appreciate the distinctions made by structuralist linguistics concerning the referent, the signifier, and the signified, he developed his concerns for isolating the human spirit and concomitantly realized that an empirical attitude could not contain this spirit but would reflect it antithetically.

This reflection had a triangular structure elaborating his early tendency toward dichotomous distinctions. The three constituents of the sign (the referent, the signified, and the signifier), as revealed by structuralist linguistics, were coincidentally analogous to the tripartite orders of the human intellect (the real, the symbolic, and the imaginary) identified by Lacan. The real and the referent, the symbol and the signified, and the imaginary and the signifier were analogous components to triangular systems involving communication. The Lacanian components of the intellect provided a psychological substratum for the linguistic triad.

The opposition of inside/outside was also a viable distinction to discuss the psycholinguistic bond between the phenomena of cultural practices and the noumena of the human spirit. The real and the referent are part of the phenomenal order, verified by the scientific empiricism that Lévi-Strauss adopted methodologically early in his investigations with ethnology. But, as always concerned with what is other or what is beyond appearances, he once again unmasked the superficiality of what appeared to be truth. The empirical method was revealed as wanting because of its singular focus on phenomena.

Lévi-Strauss developed his insights to become sensitive to what is
to be found, as Edmund Leach has told us, "not 'in' the empirical
facts themselves but 'at the back' of the empirical facts."[1] Symbols
revealed to Lévi-Strauss that there was something on the other side
of empirical data. The literal significance of things in themselves
was only part of the projection of the human spirit into the world
of phenomena.

The "back side" of empirical data was revealed by the work of
symbols to distinguish certain signs as worthy of more than literal
meaning. Similarly, the signified portion of a sign is a transitional
element in a sign because it represents something which has been
chosen to be distinct and different from other objects. Both symbols
and the signified are produced by the human spirit to make its mark
on the world of phenomena. Both are verifications that human
interaction with the empirical realm has occurred. But there is more
to this verification process, according to Lévi-Strauss. The interaction being observed may sometimes be conscious and logical. But
far more interesting to him was the interaction between the noumenal and the phenomenal, despite conscious human intentions.
There is another order where the human spirit appears to reside, or
at least to generate the whole structure or triadic network of sig-
nification and intellectual activity.

The imaginary realm is the arena where everything comes together. Here the nonconscious intellectual forces are responsible for
linking the real with the symbolic, the referent with the signified,
in ways still to be revealed. The distinction "nonconscious" is used
to speak about how Lévi-Strauss understood intellectual activity
other than consciousness. The unconscious, by contrast, was a Freudian concept adapted and modified by Lévi-Strauss. As he sought to
demonstrate how ". . . myths are thought within humanity un-
beknownst to it,"[2] he revealed in his analyses of various cultural
practices how the conscious intentions of certain peoples about their
cultural values were subverted by nonconscious patterns and drives,
thus linking them in their humanity to other peoples. These elements of the nonconscious were indicators of the common human
spirit underlying cultural differentiation and assimilation.

Probing the Depths of the Geological Model

Lévi-Strauss's geological inspiration directed him toward taking
a layered view of the human spirit. These layers implied a covering

or imbricating of humanity's intellectual core. As a result, he sought the kernel whereupon all the layers would be cast aside. The Freudian distinctions of manifest and latent behavior lent themselves very well to Lévi-Strauss's penchant for looking beyond the obvious to find a "human spirit" in all its nakedness and universality, thus revealing the emptiness of so many human prejudices and hatreds based on the appearances of human difference. The manifest intentions of peoples telling stories (myths) about themselves to justify their own conceptions about who they are were simply inadequate to Lévi-Strauss. He was intellectually suspicious and wanted "to reveal the secret springs which . . . move the human spirit."[3] The words *secret* and *springs* are especially significant because of the suggestion that there is movement below the surface which must be revealed. He sought to expose the layering process of nonconscious motivation and thus to lay bare the human spirit. For example, he analyzed myths by identifying certain latent properties such as repetition whose purpose was to make the structure of the myths manifest to him.[4] So Lévi-Strauss understood himself to have a special role, as does a psychoanalyst, in probing the psychological depths of the human psyche to find the daemon, that part of the self that gives integrity to the intellect and to its perceived world. But depth psychology and psychoanalysis were inadequate to the task because of their reliance on the center, the ego to be found at the core as an explanation of intellectual integrity.

Instead, Lévi-Strauss analyzed the functioning of the human spirit and found no core at all to sustain that celebrated goal. At the "center" there was no content to undergird his speculations about *the* human spirit. He was surprised to find that the so-called primitive peoples understood the role of the nonconscious and were able to manipulate it through their rituals and aesthetic endeavors.[5] So he had to come to terms with this nonconscious activity and adapted Lacan's neo-Freudian understanding that the unconscious is structured like language. In this scheme, the form of the unconscious is similar to the form of language in that both of them serve as conveyors of information. There is no specific place that could be perpetually identified as the source of meaning. Similarly, no matter how many layers Lévi-Strauss uncovered in the psyche of a given people, the center or core was constantly being displaced and continued to resist identification. Giving up the attempt to locate and isolate this human spirit, he instead decided to describe its functioning.[6]

In this description of noumenal functioning, the nonconscious elements were assigned major roles in the structures. Lévi-Strauss was convinced that the "primitive" peoples, who acknowledged so well the importance of nonconscious practices, were driven by their daemon to be "other" than what they wanted to be. His term "la pensée sauvage" must not be understood simply as the "mind of the primitive peoples" whom he studied but also as the intellectual common denominator for humanity. *Sauvage* means unsophisticated, primeval, and also elemental. Thus, due to the research by Lévi-Strauss, I reiterate the appreciation of one of his readers that "unsophisticated thought is not 'I am thinking' but 'the id is thinking': this thinking is hearing and corresponding."[7] By making us aware of the social (hearing) and relational (corresponding) affects of the nonconscious players in thinking, Lévi-Strauss underscored the playful nature of thought with its rules, its stakes, its goals, and the parameters of its intellectual games.

His association with structural linguistics during the 1940s in the United States gave him a penchant for isolating the components of the game of language. The Swiss linguist Saussure had spoken about language as a chess game with its players and choices. The rules were elaborated by his successors in structural linguistics. The Prague School, especially represented by Roman Jakobson to Lévi-Strauss, advocated making manifest such latent linguistic features as the dominant and recessive phonetic features mapped by Trubetskoy on a grid that looked like an accountant's balance sheet with columns of pluses and minuses. Inspired by these types of binary analyses, Lévi-Strauss set out to map "the mass of nonconscious rules [which] continue to be the most important and the most effective [in our biological inheritance]."[8] His many schematics of these rules are testimonies to the abstract, mathematical flavor of his maps. But yet it is still not clear if there is a single game or even a set of games in which intellectual players express their human spirit.

Insights into Blindness

Lévi-Strauss was intent upon making humanity see its own blindness to its organization of apparently diverse cultural identities. His revelation about the incest taboo, that it camouflages women being traded in a grand scheme to obtain social leverage among certain peoples, exemplifies his talent in flushing out deep patterns of human consciousness. The word *deep* is used deliberately here because of his inspiration by depth psychology and geology to look for explanations buried by deceptive appearances. But he soon learned that blindness can be the channeling of one's perspective so as not to see something posed at a bias from the viewer. Lévi-Strauss went so far as to say that ". . . we are seated on something or leaning against something which we can't see because we have our back against it."[9] And so his self-appointed role was to turn us around or at least to orient our point of view so we are not so blind to our own human nature's proclivity for enclosing ourselves in an edifice which we formed however unknowingly.

One such edifice whose underpinnings Lévi-Strauss has spent much time revealing is history. As I have already argued, he did not totally discard the notion of history but instead recast it in order to accommodate structuralist concepts of human thinking. A significant spinoff from his review of the parameters of human history was his development of Marx's insight that humanity makes its own history without knowing what it is doing. Lévi-Strauss would have us believe that this insight is the foundation for both history and ethnology.[10] Of course, he included the qualification that the justification for history is found in the first part of the statement (humanity makes its own history) while ethnology looks beyond the obvious in its inspiration by the second part of Marx's insight (humanity is not aware of making its own history). Of course, the French word *histoire* means both "history" and "story." This ambivalence reveals the heart of the matter for Lévi-Strauss because nonconscious storytelling is really what history is about for him, and what ethnology can reveal as part of the mythology of the social sciences, so long concerned with being identified with the "scientific method."

The blindness inherent in our human proclivity for narration is especially exemplified in the ethnological studies of so-called primitive peoples. Lévi-Strauss would have us believe that the primitive mind offers an intellectual model, although less abstract and more concrete in its address, for humanity to study. Likewise, the nonconscious elements play a significant, if different, role in structuring storytelling. He observed that "the so-called primitive societies recognize with more objectivity than we do the role of nonconscious activity in aesthetic creation and manipulate with astonishing clairvoyance this obscure life of the human spirit."[11] The lesson to be learned is that the mysterious side of the human spirit should be allowed to express itself through these narrative exercises involved in the cultural identification of a people. And the "mystery" has everything to do with our inner humanity and what we don't know that we are doing. Lévi-Strauss encouraged us to come to terms with this inner voice of the daemonic or nonconscious self which is either controlled by or controls the direction of the human spirit.

A Dynamic Disequilibrium

The control of the human spirit is demonstrated by Lévi-Strauss's analyses of various cultural taboos and myths. He showed that the nonconscious factors in human thinking had to be flushed to the surface so that peoples can be in better control of their own fate by being aware of how the nonconscious directs what they consciously claim to be doing. He pointed out that, whereas consciousness makes claims for coherence, "the nonconscious infrasystem is dynamic and unbalanced since it is concomitantly constituted by the legacy of the past and the future tendencies not yet realized."[12] So the temporal struggle of the analyst like Lévi-Strauss entails the coherence of the conscious present with the unbalanced fluidity of the nonconscious past and future. Structuralist history was thus formed as the anthropologist strove to flush the bubbling components of the nonconscious into present consciousness.

Wherever the French ethnologist looked for these nonconscious components, he always found a decentralizing and fragmented activity. This resistance to being dominated by the conscious present was in the very subject matter. The centering ego of peoples could not be found. All Lévi-Strauss could find were fragments of myths throughout the world. No unifying human spirit willingly revealed its core. Here and there, as with tribal masks or with the incest taboo, insights could be made into the theoretical coherence between nonconscious structures and apparent conscious aims. But even here, he did not reveal once and for all the consistent ties between the two realms of activity.

Instead, he reified the Lacanian triadic operants, especially the existence of the imaginary in bridging the gap between the real and the symbolic orders of human communication. The imaginary is the intellectual activity that structures or organizes particles of truth within us and links them with the outside. Lévi-Strauss identified the existence of this activity through his explorations of the nonconscious structures in human thinking. Even though the artifacts he analyzed were phenomena culturally or socially conditioned, such as totemic beliefs, he continued to maintain that "if the illusion contains a particle of truth, this is not outside us but within us."[13] So his work was dedicated to getting beyond the illusion, to discovering the pattern beneath conscious motivation, and to stipulating the particle of truth with contrived formulas that most of us cannot read. And there is wisdom to all this because of his skepticism about the obvious and his continual struggle with searching for those elusive particles. The wisdom was in the method not in the end-product.

Emptiness at the Core

Once Lévi-Strauss started poking around in the arena of that middle ground between conscious and nonconscious activity, he soon realized that there was no space nor substance to the nonconscious. The analyst is thus left with an activity once described by Roland Barthes at Johns Hopkins in 1967 as the peeling of an onion, the lifting of successive layers or folds only to be left with nothing at the center.

But Lévi-Strauss was not frustrated by this realization. In fact, it became one of the bases for his structuralist enterprise. He would have us understand that "the nonconscious is always empty . . . [and] it is restricted to imposing structural laws, which exhaust its reality, on inarticulated elements which originate elsewhere."[14] Hence, the "nonconscious" is not so much a thing as it is an activity of organizing nonconscious factors into some sort of cohesion. Since emptiness characterizes the center, this cohesion is innately conditioned by the laws of its gathering activity. The elements being gathered do originate elsewhere and magnetically adhere to the human spirit. Lévi-Strauss was involved in separating out the rules by which the "magnetism" selected and then ordered the particles into culturally acceptable types of cohesion. The emptiness at the core had to be filled naturally. The way it was filled concerned Claude Lévi-Strauss.

It has been observed that Lévi-Strauss was so enamored of "structures" that he modified the workings of the unconscious to suit his model. Paul Ricoeur especially took exception to the creation of "a nonconsciousness of forms, a categorical nonconscious,"[15] which lent itself so well to being mapped out by esoteric mathematical abstractions. Because of this level of abstraction, Ricoeur accusingly pointed his finger to "the Kantian nonconsciousness of Lévi-Strauss."[16] The abstract model was driving Lévi-Strauss in his assumptions about nonconscious activity, according to Ricoeur. And indeed the human spirit was an idealistic concept toward which Lévi-Strauss has strived throughout his writings.

However, we should not simply dismiss the insights of Lévi-Strauss into nonconscious activity because of their limitations. Even Ricoeur stipulated that, despite a Kantian nonconsciousness, the structuralism of Lévi-Strauss does make us realize that organization does entail systematizing without our being aware of it.[17] In addition, Ricoeur developed his "hermeneutic" approach largely in contrast to what Lévi-Strauss was doing. So the work of Lévi-Strauss in the area of the nonconscious was also important as a foil and even a catalyst to hermeneutic studies into the relationships between symbolic activity and the unconscious.

Alternatives to Measuring and Counting

The scientific spirit that so inspired Lévi-Strauss in his early years as an ethnologist led him to consider alternate ways of understanding the concept "scientific." The nonconscious factors in human thinking intrigued the philosophically trained young graduate from the Sorbonne. Although he appeared to espouse an empirical model for anthropology, his *Tristes tropiques* revealed an impressionistic mind that was largely intuitive and concerned with the lines of demarcation between nature and culture, native and foreign, primitive and sophisticated, and especially between one ethnic identity and another.

Rather than measuring and counting the components of nonconscious cultural artifacts, he assigned to the scientific spirit a sense of grouping or isolating modes of thinking. This grouping activity led him to look at nontraditional manners of understanding nonconscious operants in human behavior. Not restricted by spatial or temporal data, he sketched abstract spaces bounded only by the parameters of the structural laws he identified. In effect, his work of identifying the patterns of the nonconscious mind and then translating them into mathematical formulas and equations exemplifies for us today the very intellectual structuring he sought to discover among the various peoples of the world. As Edward Said pointed out, Lévi-Strauss would have us believe that the nonconscious demonstrates classification as "the primary activity of the mind."[18] But there is more to the contributions of Lévi-Strauss. The classification performed by the mind is a human activity, and the human part of his insights has been too long ignored by his readers. Let us turn then to the "humanism" fostered and perpetuated by the writings of Lévi-Strauss and examine what it is that made it so human and at the same time so little recognized.

Chapter Ten

A New Humanism

A Philosophical or Scientific Approach to Humanistic Study?

All of these various issues that arise from the writings of Claude Lévi-Strauss lead us to the central issue: does his work further the interests of humanity? He claims ethnology or social anthropology as a "human science."[1] But many of his contemporaries are wary of what he means by the term *human* because his inspiration from the scientific method and the abstract, mathematical flavor of his analyses clearly align his studies with the natural sciences. His was no humanistic flavor in ethnology. Instead, his background in philosophy at the Sorbonne brought an understanding of *human* in the context of Renaissance humanism, that very specific search for what is human through the pursuit of the Latin and Greek models of culture. This is not to say that Lévi-Strauss was modeling the human spirit on the Renaissance man nor that he was necessarily intent upon Greek or Latin mythology. But he was intent upon revealing the nature of human communication, semiosis, in cultural practices. Recalling the Greimas definition of semiotics as the study of how humanity conceives, organizes, and humanizes its world, we project Lévi-Strauss in the middle of this enterprise with his contributions in ethnology.

Renaissance erudition was not an accidental forerunner when Lévi-Strauss pronounced that the goal of ethnology was "to spread humanism to all humanity."[2] Earlier in his career, he had stated quite clearly that "ethnology . . . consists in the scientific aspect of all research concerning humanity."[3] These are grandiose schemes for a discipline still in its infancy. He had no clear conception of what this new humanism would be like, but he did realize that the rules of structure in human thinking, as I discussed in chapter 1, pointed to a humanistic model that transcended monocultural and hegemonic boundaries, as I elaborated in chapter 2. While he pursued a definition of the human spirit under the pseudoscientific guise of mathematical formulas and logic, some of his colleagues took exception to his leadership role as a humanist. Sanche de Gramont was so vocal about it as to proclaim that "with Lévi-Strauss, the whole humanist tradition goes down the drain."[4] I should qualify that opinion with the fact that the Renaissance humanists were concerned with isolating human interests and debunking the halo effect of religious explanations of the world. So, too, Lévi-Strauss set about to debunk the incest taboo, religious myths, totemism, etc., to demonstrate the universal human phenomenon of story-telling. In his explanation of his interest in Jean-Jacques Rousseau, the French ethnologist told us that, in the eighteenth century, "that age of myths, the only humanity [Rousseau] had, made a slave of him."[5] That insight into Rousseau is likewise applicable to one that Lévi-Strauss had of all humanity: that we are blind to ourselves because our very nature causes us to narrate stories in which we invest belief despite our conscious designs. So Lévi-Strauss would reveal our humanity to us despite ourselves.

Women in Exchange

His studies of kinship theory and the incest taboo were especially revealing in this regard. Whereas intricate schemes had been previously devised to explain the conscious aims of kinship systems and the prohibition of incest, Lévi-Strauss looked below the surface and discovered the phenomenon that women had become the universal economic means for creating and sustaining human relationships. We were blinded by elaborate schemes of our kinship habits so that we could not see what a student of Lévi-Strauss has called "the essence of humanity."[6]

What Lévi-Strauss offered, however, was no humanistic view of women as human beings. Instead, we witnessed his elaboration of the idea of women as dehumanized objects of barter. A woman had no personality in his presentation of her distinctive role among cultures of different kinds. Like himself, however, women were placed on the outside looking in, differentiated by hostile power groups. Once again the outside/inside distinction worked, this time to portray women as excluded from human identity, or, as Lévi-Strauss observed, "the caste systems understood women to be naturally heterogeneous, and the totemic groups understood them to be culturally heterogeneous."[7] So the perceived differences of women from men led to their isolation and eventual "objectification" outside humanity. Lévi-Strauss would qualify his observation by noting that women were similar to men naturally as sharing in humanity; but societies created various systems to distinguish them, whether in matriarchal or in patriarchal settings. One cannot help but notice that Lévi-Strauss is himself part of the cultural determination of women's lot, as exemplified in the tone of his analyses of their role in myths. I refer, for example, to his pessimism about woman's periodic nature and her consequent need to be educated or "corrected" by man.[8] He was not comfortable with woman in an ethnological setting and needed to point out her liabilities as a narrative subject in the myths of various peoples: "woman, being eternally opossum and vixen, is incapable of overcoming her contradictory nature and realizing perfection."[9] His tone here is questionable because the implication is that the male human being *is* perfectible! Woman's reality as a human being within the fold of humanity appeared to be glossed over in his search for the human spirit.

And yet contemporary feminist writers do point out his discovery of the economic "objectification" of women. Jane Gallop, for example, cites this insight by Lévi-Strauss as the major contribution of structuralism to feminist thought.[10] Georges Bataille had noted in 1957 that women are thus understood as "objects of generosity" since theirs is the fate of being vehicles of "communication," understood on the level of social and cultural exchange. However, Bataille took exception to generosity because the facts of each situation gave incontrovertible weight to the self-interest of such trade on the part of the males in each society.[11] Lévi-Strauss seemed to have revealed only the tip of the iceberg and did not sound very convincing to those women, upset by his systematizing their existence in an economic model, when he replaced women with men, a little too easily: "the female reader . . . can easily find support in the assurance that the rules of the game would remain unchanged should it be decided to consider the men as being exchanged by women's groups."[12] He would have been better advised to develop his insights about the economic role assigned to women in relation to his concerns about racism, a social and political problem in which his humanistic training could have had significant impact.

Lévi-Strauss has often viewed humanity within the framework of progress and its parameters. His United Nations pamphlet *Race et histoire* portrayed racism from the perspective of cultural relativism and the need for neighbors to differentiate themselves from one another. Raymond Aron took Lévi-Strauss to task for not logically castigating racists because the effect of not doing so was to allow the racist mentality to project a regressive concept of humanity.[13] And yet Lévi-Strauss had insisted upon a holistic view of humanity progressively developing from its diversity in cultural and political units: "Humanity becomes one, identical to itself; but, this unity and identity can only be realized progressively and the variety of cultures illustrates the moments in the process. . . ."[14] Similarly, the problems of progress and racism were not brought together in his treatment of kinship and women. A certain mythologizing of the role of women precluded his introduction of racism and humanistic progress into his observations. Although he spent much of his career revealing the subtle narratives we narrate nonconsciously, he himself was also spinning a yarn about the economic structure of women in society. There was no sense of change or variability in development in his theory of the exchange of women within kinship systems.

And yet, within the Lévi-Strauss ethnological framework, women were also communicators as well as the ones being communicated. He did realize, after some pressure from feminist circles, that "woman is nevertheless a person, and . . . insofar as she is understood as a sign, we must recognize in her a producer of signs."[15] She is not totally dependent upon man. Instead, woman cooperated in the creation and maintenance of the symbols and parameters upon which the need for trading her was based. In the kinship studies by Lévi-Strauss, we note his recovery of matrilineal systems whereby the very identities of the societies are founded upon the women who give their names to the livelihood of their people. In various totemic societies, for example, the matrilineal groups were clearly distinguished from patrilineal systems by the qualities associated with each one, as Lévi-Strauss identified them: "matrilineal totemism attests the diachronic and biological continuity of the clan; it is the flesh and blood perpetuated from generation to generation by the women of the lineage; while patrilineal totemism expresses local solidarity."[16] The women in the matrilineal systems were actively involved in communicating themselves to future generations and receiving the communications from other women of their lineage. The contrasts between the matrilineal and the patrilineal kinship systems provide us with humanistic lessons about the dangers of unilateral thinking in trapping peoples with prejudicial behavioral patterns leading to injustices of all sorts.

The Ethnocentric Prison

Perhaps the greatest lesson Lévi-Strauss learned from his studies of racism was the threat posed by provincialism to political neighbors. In his presentation of racism, the tendency of neighbors to differentiate and then isolate from each other leads to refusals to understand one another. Political and cultural chauvinism then develops along with blindness to the arbitrary nature of human differences. Intolerance for differences often results from condescension by one neighbor toward another. His own life was a mirror of these situations: Jewish/Gentile, Belgian/French, ethnologist/scientist, soldier/expatriate, etc. So the universal racist problem of self/other was also the microcosm/macrocosm of Lévi-Strauss and the world around him. But he refused to see the problem as an existential or a phenomenological setting for the self in a hostile world. Instead, we should recall a previously cited passage that alludes to the problem of the human prison: "humanity invests itself in monoculture; it is prepared to mass-produce civilization, just like the sugar beet."[17] Of course, this tendency toward homogenization is also the threat of incest within a family, group, people, culture, political unit, etc.

Lévi-Strauss did advocate heterogeneity as a healthy posture to preclude the dangers of racist hegemony. His geometric sensitivity induced him to model human nature across sexual, ethnic, and political grounds. The algebraic underpinnings of this geometric understanding gave him a sense of the inability of social boundaries to enclose or limit human striving for perfection. One of his readers went so far as to portray the lesson from the French ethnologist thus: "One must get out of one's own family to be truly human and to discover the human; otherwise a non-human, incestuous, withdrawn introversion results."[18] Looking toward difference, rather than away from it, thus becomes a way to preclude the traps set by monocultural thinking.

Although Lévi-Strauss did present a rather intensive study of kinship, he had a much more expansive perspective concerning the context of families within groups. Families are composed and aligned through social and cultural factors that influence the decisions of individuals. So Lévi-Strauss proceeded to identify the structural ties between families and their societies. He told Sanche de Gramont at one point that he had no sympathy for the century in which he was living because of the assertions of "the total ascendancy of man over nature and of certain forms of humanity over others."[19] So he sought ways to discourage the condescension of one group to another and explored models of relationships not implying superiority or inferiority.

Societies isolated from mainstream "civilizations" provided him with exotic samples of how to escape the trap of monoculture while retaining a humanistic identity. He went to great lengths to talk around the concept of "the primitive or savage mind," as if it existed independently of a "civilized mind." He argued against Sartre's dialectical practice and stipulated that the "savage mind" was distinct in the anecdotal and geometrical fashion of expressing itself. Hence, the education provided by mainstream civilizations inculcated weltanschauungs that impeded the appreciation of how isolated societies thought. The challenge for the ethnologist, as for all of us, was to learn to become "the other." In order to analyze the ways of doing this, Lévi-Strauss knew very well that "we cannot remain imprisoned in the heart of another society."[20] So he compared and contrasted phenomena from heterogeneous groups in order to identify patterns and similarities capable of creating a case for the common bonds of the human spirit.

The division of labor is an intriguing example of a problem universal to all peoples working together in a group and offering some commentary on our human nature. Jean-Jacques Rousseau had superficially conjectured that labor was assigned in the state of nature according to the sexes. Lévi-Strauss set the record straight with his cross-cultural studies by distinguishing the universal fact of the division of work and the "modalities" by which some societies assign work according to predisposed talents assigned arbitrarily to one sex or to the other.[21]

Such insights by Lévi-Strauss lead us today to the conjecture that the human problem of racism is culturally affected. He would have us believe that "race . . . is a function among others of culture."[22] So the distinctions made by peoples about ethnic groups are arbitrary judgments of differentiation. The traps made by these culturally affected decisions often encircle the decision-makers in monocultural

isolation. Instead, Lévi-Strauss advocated a humane program of tolerance, which was not simply an intellectual position, dispensing
favors of acceptance now and then to one group or to another. It is
"a dynamic attitude which consists in foreseeing, understanding,
and stirring up in advance what must be."[23] As I indicated in
chapters 4, 7, and 9, this "dynamism" is significant because of the
biological and geological models advocating the accommodation of
change and transformation. He realized that static attitudes were
forms of human imprisonment in themselves. His vision of a dynamic tolerance would recognize cultural differences and respect the
distinctions of outside/inside as viable principles of human identity.

Ethnology as the Guardian of Humanism

The tolerance advocated by Lévi-Strauss was promoted through
his humanistic agenda for ethnological research. Indeed, it has been
observed that he began his career with the goal of placing "ethnology
as the guardian angel of a certain type of humanism."[24] A "guardian
angel" wards off evil tendencies; and so, in this capacity, ethnology
had a moral agenda to guide society away from its ethnocentric
tendencies with all the potential racism of such ideological single-
mindedness. This was a "dynamic" view of tolerance in that ethnology would be constantly reminding us of our need for recognizing
diversity in the ethnic and cultural parameters of human thinking.
This "idealistic" role for ethnology was proposed by a young Lévi-
Strauss not yet involved in tangles with either Sartre or Ricoeur
about what was at stake in this humanism. And some of his British
colleagues in anthropology (e.g. Evans Pritchard, Edmund Leach)
were not so sanguine about the "humanistic" role for their discipline.
To be fair to the French ethnologist, it must be pointed out that
he advocated alliances among the natural sciences (the scientific
method) and the humanities (the recognition of differentiation) with
ethnology. Lévi-Strauss was not proposing that there be a merger
of ethnology into either of these areas. At an early point in his
career, he criticized Pritchard for recommending the divisions of
social and cultural anthropology for fear that social anthropology
would be jeopardized by being consigned to the "camp of the
humanities"[25] rather than to the social sciences. In France, the
division "human sciences" is used rather than social sciences and

aligns those disciplines much closer to the humanities by their very name.

Nevertheless, Lévi-Strauss advanced the notion that ethnology had to play a leadership role in pointing out our common human spirit and in concomitantly recognizing the importance of differentiation while avoiding ethnocentrism. But he did not see himself as a philosopher. Although some of his anthropological colleagues tend to emphasize the philosophical overtones of his analyses (e.g., E. Leach's *Claude Lévi-Strauss,* 1970), Lévi-Strauss preferred to see himself differently: "I did not want to create a philosophy; I simply tried to become aware, for my personal profit, of the philosophical implications of certain aspects of my work."[26] Despite himself and his intentions, he involved ethnology in major philosophical battles during the 1960s because of his moral charge for its endeavors. Many could not understand how his mathematical formulas could be as morally directed as he would have them be. And so Sartre and Ricoeur, soon followed by many another respected humanist, took Lévi-Strauss to task for his self-imposed role for ethnology. Lévi-Strauss responded with gusto. But his vision was a bit tainted by his opinion of the dominance of mainstream Western civilization. In reply to Sartre, for example, he quipped that "Hell is ourselves"[27] in obvious reference to the existentialist motto from *Les Mouches* that "Hell is the others." He thus exemplifies a certain contempt for himself as part of a system that was supposed to be exemplary to others. Jacques Derrida, who has become a similar type of cult figure for the substitute to structuralism in deconstructionism, understood the problem within the discourse of Lévi-Strauss: "The only weakness in the handiwork [bricolage] . . . is its inability to justify itself from part to part in its own discourse."[28] In other words, the cohesion of a philosophical system appears to be absent in the work of Lévi-Strauss. Despite his postulates of a "human spirit" and the necessity for dynamic tolerance, there is a lack of cohesion in presenting a positive vision of humanity throughout his work. "Structuralism," as he advocated it, did give us examples of how the human mind universally creates organic patterns and models; but it was not a positive force in proposing cohesive ways to improve our behavior. Yvan Simonis would go so far as to say that it was "inept at thinking humanism in a positive manner."[29] However limited may have been his theoretical contributions, Claude Lévi-

Strauss did nevertheless contribute to humanism, but poetically
rather than philosophically.

A Poetics of Difference

In *Tristes tropiques,* Lévi-Strauss was an impressionistic, almost
poetic intellectual who portrayed the isolated peoples of Brazil in a
Rousseauvian image of lost innocence. Because of the popularity of
that work, he was understood by many of his colleagues in anthropology to be a misguided scientist, too concerned with poetics and
not enough with the scientific methods of investigation and verification. For example, Neville Dyson-Hudson put forward "a suspicion that Lévi-Strauss's analyses add up to a poetics for social
anthropology, rather than a theory in any scientific sense."[30] "Poetics" must be understood here to mean fragmented, rather than
cohesive, glimpses into what the study of socialized humanity could
offer.

For Lévi-Strauss, this poetics provides us with models about the
alternation of similarity and difference. Gilles Deleuze provided an
important philosophical treatise (*La Différence et la répétition,* 1967)
about these principles. But Lévi-Strauss demonstrated why these
principles are important to improve our cultural and social situations. His constant reminder of the "human spirit" which we all
share was especially crucial to his UNESCO study on racism. And
despite the importance of "dynamic tolerance" to invigorate this
"spirit," he also pointed out that "many customs are born . . .
from the single desire not to remain the same in relationship to a
neighboring group which submitted to a specific rite a domain that
had not been dreamed of as being . . . regulated."[31] These insights,
though interspersed and fragmented throughout his work, do give
us a better understanding of our human nature.

For some, "poetics" also implies a scientific model by which we
can bring diverse elements together. And I have already remarked
that Lévi-Strauss did try to introduce scientific methods to ethnology, perhaps in reply to the critique of his impressionistic style in
Tristes tropiques. Some think that this adaptation of a scientific model
was merely "curious."[32] But we must remember his training at the
Sorbonne, where Gaston Bachelard had an enormous influence during that period when Lévi-Strauss was enrolled. Bachelard's *Nouvel*

esprit scientifique (1934), for example, expounded the idea that "sooner or later, the scientific spirit will become the fundamental theme of philosophical polemics: this thought will lead us to substitute an objectively rectified discursive metaphysics for an intuitive and immediate metaphysics."[33] It was the "objectively rectified" that led Lévi-Strauss throughout his career to search for ethnological samples, gathered by other anthropologists for the most part, corroborating his insights into humanity. Since he was primarily an ethnographer who wrote about rather than visited peoples throughout the world, it was no coincidence that he found his scientific model in mathematics because of its abstract nature and also its humanistic origins. Those origins were not obvious ones but were described by him thus: "it was toward man, much more than toward the physical world, that the first geometrists and arithmeticians oriented their speculations."[34] With this sympathy of mathematics toward humanity and the affinity between mathematics and music, Lévi-Strauss constructed his various models and formulas relating myths, customs, and artifacts, of which his "poetics" is loosely made.

The affinity between music and human thinking was an especially obsessive matter for Lévi-Strauss. Organic structure was learned from biology, and then the notions of rhythm and harmony added direction and cohesion to provide models for how thinking is formed and organized. His analyses of myths, especially in *Le Cru et le cuit,* were inspired by musical motifs and were reliant upon musical models for explaining the construction of these stories. The mathematical precision of musical notation united with the humanistic pursuit of song and dance to provide a potentially rich discipline from which to learn how to link science and humanism. Likewise, he had proposed that ethnology could offer "the means to bridge the gap between a philosophical and a scientific approach to the study of man."[35] By "philosophical" here he meant a Kantian ideal which contrasted with a biologically or empirically based understanding of human nature. Music gave him the inspiration for a rhythmic approach to blending information gleaned from all other disciplines because he projected ethnology as the place where "the scientific aspect of all research concerning man"[36] could be performed. That "scientific" filter had the specific format of an emerging field of study called "semiotics"—the science of communication—whereby his work pointed to the future.

Anthropological Semiotics

When Lévi-Strauss referred to Hell as ourselves, his insight was not so much philosophical as it was semiotic. Like his intellectual forefather, Jean-Jacques Rousseau, Lévi-Strauss was keenly aware of the human dilemma in communication—that we are prisoners of our subjectivity, governed by our nonconscious selves despite our drives to communicate with others in diverse manners. Through his presentation of this dilemma in analyses of various ethnological topics, he has made a case for what A. J. Greimas, one of the most influential contemporary French semioticians, has called "anthro-pological semiotics."[37] This subspecialty of semiotics focuses upon human rather than natural communication and enlists the aid of anthropology to identify the subtle ways human beings communicate to one another in various cultural and social settings. Lévi-Strauss was instrumental in pointing to the recognition of respecting the diversity of complex ways that people use to communicate to one another. His ethnological studies of myths, totemism, masks, re-ligions, and taboos were intended by him to probe the common nature of the human spirit. Ironically, the studies remain as testi-monies to his observation that "exchanges which are too easy equalize and confound"[38] human diversity.

Lévi-Strauss also claimed for ethnology those areas of semiotics not covered by linguistics. These include mythic language, oral signs, gestures, and marriage rules. However, some of these do overlap into the linguistic concern with verbal signs. So his claim did extend into the discipline of linguistics, whose influence during the 1940s has already been mentioned several times. He in fact adapted the concerns of linguistics with signs to the anthropological prospectus for humanity: "Human beings communicate through symbols and signs; for anthropology, which is a conversation be-tween human beings, anything positioned as the intermediary be-tween two objects is symbol and sign."[39] It is that "conversation" that so compelled him to be an ethnologist because in that discipline he was able to observe the physical links among the various people of the world. The rites, the practices, the taboos, the unwritten laws all bespeak a conversation innate to human beings, at once distinguishing them and uniting them.

Claude Lévi-Strauss did realize that the human spirit was a choir of many voices. Although he did seek unanimity in the organic

structure of human thinking, eventually he realized that the recognition of the diversity and a tolerance for it was far more worth-
while than a single ideological framework. As he struggled with
complicated formulas to translate the "noise" or the "je ne sais quoi"
of cultural practices, he gave us commentaries on the alterity and
the uniqueness of the human condition.

Two final citations together provide us with testimony for the
epitaph to this French ethnographer. As a demythologizer, he was
ironically the myth-maker of nonconscious designs as he reconsti-
tuted myths for others. My first citation for his epitaph is a prospectus from *La Pensée sauvage* about the human spirit, which he
spent his ethnographic life trying to totalize, as he would say: "We
believe that the ultimate goal of the social sciences is not to constitute
humanity, but to dissolve it."[40] In that dissolution of the single,
hegemonic unit called humanity, Lévi-Strauss gave us a celebration
of human differences and the similarities within which he personally
struggled for his identity to be an insider rather than an outsider.
The second citation is from Honoré de Balzac, the nineteenth-
century realist who foresaw the arrival of Lévi-Strauss and to whom
the French ethnographer himself referred, perhaps ironically com-
menting on himself: "Ideas are a complete system inside of us,
similar to one of the kingdoms of nature, a kind of flowering whose
iconography will be outlined by a genius who will be renowned as
a fool, perhaps."[41]

Chapter Eleven
Conclusion

We have come full circle with Claude Lévi-Strauss. Perhaps it is better to call it a vortex that we have traveled because the French ethnographer did not simply retrace his steps. From his neo-Cartesian tendency to bifurcate the universe into polarities, he projected a new humanism in which a dynamic view of tolerance would be a key principle. He did not abandon his dualistic vision, largely inspired by his concern with the inside/outside dialectic. This perspective began with his own personal condition and eventually entailed the choices that all peoples make in differentiating themselves from their neighbors while creating their own identities. The racist problem of monocultural thinking was a lifelong struggle with which he contended.

The linguistic inspiration of a binary system led Lévi-Strauss into a career-long association with Roman Jakobson. Their analysis of Baudelaire's poem served to identify Lévi-Strauss with the term "structuralism," borrowed from the structural linguistics of the Prague School. The superficial application of dualism to textual pairs was quickly disparaged by literary opponents of this "scientific" posture for literary criticism. But Lévi-Strauss quickly learned that the opposition between appearances and substance, or between manifest and latent truths, would provide more viable and credible results for his method.

His work was characterized by a suspicion about the viability of appearances. With a geological sense for exploring the substrata, he contrasted manifest and latent truths to reveal unsuspected harmonies among ritual and cultural practices throughout the world. Dissatisfied with form as an explanation for the coherence between appearances and substance, Lévi-Strauss sought a dynamic type of glue that could explain the modulated rhythms of storytelling as a universal phenomenon in cultural and ritual practices.

Another physical science, biology, provided him with the vital model for this dynamic glue. Structure became a viable concept for Lévi-Strauss because it offered the possibility of explaining the relationships between the parts and the whole in any story or myth. The four latent properties of a structure were also well-suited for explaining the vital and rejuvenative character of storytelling. These properties were its potential for transformation, its predictable features, the changing relationships of its elements, and its accountability for all the facts. In order to discover these properties, however, one had to learn the system or the network by which the parts of the story related to the whole story. The system was accessed through the "atom" of a structure, that is, the interconnection explaining the relationships among the components of the whole being analyzed. This interconnection was characterized by Lévi-Strauss by its reciprocity among the components, its conformity to the laws of these components reacting one to another, and the performance of the practices as social gifts within a given cultural milieu.

All of these properties contributed to understanding the storyteller as a "bricoleur," a handyman doing feats of intellectual handiwork. Lévi-Strauss was also acting as a handyman himself because, as Catherine Clément pointed out, he, too, was an "interpreter of myths." So did the structure contribute to the science of ethnology? In fact it did by providing a grid upon which Lévi-Strauss could lay out his vision for the network of myths within the universal rubric of the human spirit. As I pointed out in chapter 3, he hermeneutically embodied what Ricoeur told us Lévi-Strauss was doing: making sense out of the non-sense in the apparently disjointed myths of peoples separated geographically and temporally throughout the world. Similar to the healers or shamans of isolated cultures, Lévi-Strauss saw through myths to identify the cohesion they provided for humanity. More than the common beliefs of peoples in the self-identity provided by these stories, the cohesion was achieved by the coincidence of history and ethnology in continuing the handiwork of the storytellers by uniting tribal past and present in myths.

In comparing and contrasting heterogeneous myths, this French armchair-ethnologist projected his own identity crisis through the issues of translation and treachery. Trained as a philosopher, he adopted ethnology as his own and translated his Belgian and French beginnings into French and American language exposés of other cultures. He wanted to get beyond racial prejudices fostered by political insiders who focused on the differences found in appearances. Instead, he sought the common human denominators in myths. The problem of the treachery in transposing these common denominators from their cultural milieus to the arena of the human spirit was attenuated by his modeling, which theoretically isolated the inner core of each myth, similar in his mind to variations of the same musical score. My discussion of modeling especially noted his grammatical modeling of myths. Lévi-Strauss maintained that myths could be modeled on sentence structure in that he sought economy of explanation, unity of solution, and the recognition of the whole story from one of its supposed fragments. Through pursuing the analysis of myths guided by these principles, he proposed to reduce some of the treachery inherent in translating the myths and also to account for the phenomenon of transformation.

Claude Lévi-Strauss was not a structuralist who adhered to a mere taxonomy of cultural practices or to a simple formulary reduction of peoples to a mathematical entity. Instead, his function as a structuralist was to present how rules are translated by the human spirit into cultural practices, and to use the lessons of psychoanalysis to probe the disparity between appearances and substances. As he explained the human need to express similar messages with different codes (for example, the incest taboo as an apparently unique code for repeating the control of women's lives as economic exchange), he demonstrated that the rules for the structuring of the codes were aligned in a geometrical space composed of axes linking the apparently heterogeneous cultural practices. In the final analysis, those axes show us that human language is constantly substituting one thing for another, exemplifying the resourcefulness of humanity despite the tension of the hegemony imposed by the distinctions nature and culture.

Lévi-Strauss managed to place the terms *nature* and *culture* on the same planes of logical comprehension. He did this by demonstrating that the innate cohesion associated with nature and the mediation between humanity and the world attributed to culture are not mutually exclusive. He proposed that these terms be methodological points of reference and engaged Sartre in a debate about an artificial cosmic dichotomy between the dialectical model of thinking espoused by the Sartrean intellectual and the totalizing spirit experienced by the isolated tribal thinker. Lévi-Strauss argued that the "homo faber," or tool-maker, was just as resourceful in thinking as the sophisticated intellectual because both of them were "bricoleurs" or handymen who used the same framework of human logic, coinhabitants of what Martin Heidegger called "the House of Being" in *Sein und Zeit* (1927).

Myths also entailed nonconscious conceptions of time without progress or origins. Lévi-Strauss revealed the hegemony of Western civilization, especially through its version of history, in portraying time as linear progress from nature to culture. Instead, he would have us consider the biological and geological conceptions of time. From the biological model of mutations, we learn about nonlinear development in leaps and bounds. From the stratigraphical accounts of geological formation, Lévi-Strauss studied the art of revealing mutations below the surface of what appeared to be. By combining these scientific models, he challenged history and proposed "structuralist history" to study time as a story or myth about concatenated events and stories of people. Once again, he went beyond the appearances of time to arrive at substance through studying the symbolic manifestations of history.

The symbol provided Lévi-Strauss with the opportunity to explain the importance of appearances. Rather than a pejorative view of the deceptive character of pretense, appearances found renewed life in the context of symbolic representation because the sign was thus linked to something other than what it was: the human core, that elusive "spirit" to which Lévi-Strauss dedicated his work. From isolated tribes, he learned the healing power of masks. Similarly, the sign masked symbolic fields by which humanity could gain access to another world, the supernatural. In this realm, Lévi-Strauss constructed human intellectual matrices linking symbolic systems but never specifying the human spirit in its core. The insight of his research into symbolic representation is to reveal that there is no core beneath all the layers of semiotic representation.

As Lévi-Strauss examined various types of symbolic representation among cultural practices, he observed that symbols were privileged signs. The privilege was not a priority for written or oral systems, but an access between an individual and humanity. He helped us to recognize that symbolic representation gives us a privileged access to an internal homology, the realm of human meaning operating oblivious of deliberate intention, the nonconscious.

With a geological model of the human spirit, he examined the triangular bonding of the real, the imaginary, and the symbolic. As he uncovered successive layers of human representation, his stratigraphic model resembled more and more an onion because there was no core at the center. Instead, he found fragmentation and an absence of unity in the human mind as it classified various signs and symbols into cultural practices.

The opus of Lévi-Strauss has revealed a new humanism by demonstrating how the mind classifies in cross-cultural ways, thus revealing the semiotic nature of humanity. His writings did not constitute a philosophy. However, there are philosophical implications in his observations of how humanity conceives of, organizes, and humanizes its world. Thanks to his analysis of the incest taboo, we are now more aware of how men projected women outside their humanity. Similarly, we are also more aware of how racism has grown through an intolerance for difference. His fascination with monoculture grew out of his own insecurity with being on the outside as a Belgian, a Jew, an expatriate, an ethnologist. He lived under the tyranny of hegemony and thus understood the threat of provincialism and colonialism on humanity.

His proposal for a dynamic tolerance created a poetics of difference whereby humanity could and still can achieve a spirit of openness that transcends political boundaries. Ironically for some of his critics, Claude Lévi-Strauss achieved a certain elitist following with his structuralism. He finished his professional life on the inside looking out. From that position of power, he continued to insist that semiotics and anthropology together could bear witness to the choir of human voices. Ultimately, we can say that he brought those two disciplines together. His successors will reveal the rhythm and harmony of the music made by their interplay.

Notes and References

(Author is Claude Lévi-Strauss unless otherwise indicated)

Preface

1. A. J. Greimas, *Du Sens* (Paris: Larousse, 1970), 31.
2. Luc de Heusch, "Anthropologie structurale et le symbolisme," *Cahiers internationaux de symbolisme* (1963):51.

Chapter One

1. "Réponses à quelques questions," *Esprit,* 322 (November 1963):633: "Je n'ai pas voulu faire une philosophie."
2. Ibid., 648: "nous sommes prisonniers de la subjectivité."
3. Edmund R. Leach, *Claude Lévi-Strauss* (New York: Viking, 1970), 13.
4. *La Voie des masques* (Paris: Plon, 1979), 147.
5. Jacques Derrida, "Nature, culture, ecriture," *Cahiers pour l'analyse* 4 (September–October 1966):7.
6. Herbert R. Lottman, *Albert Camus* (New York: George Braziller, 1980), 377 ff.
7. Ibid., 386.
8. Lionel Abel, "Sartre vs. Lévi-Strauss," *Commonweal* 84, no. 13 (17 June 1966):366.
9. Paul Ricoeur, "Structure et herméneutique," *Esprit* 31 (November 1963):600.
10. *L'Homme nu* (Paris: Plon, 1971), 573: "On peut même se demander si ce prétendu structuralisme n'est pas pour servir d'alibi à l'insupportable ennui qu'exsudent les lettres contemporaines."
11. Edmund R. Leach, "Lévi-Strauss: Anthropologist and Philosopher," *New Left Review* 34 (November 1965):15.
12. Leach, *Lévi-Strauss,* 3.
13. Edmund R. Leach, *The Structural Study of Myth and Totemism* (London: Tavistock, 1967), xvii.
14. *L'Homme nu,* 566: "Ces tableaux sont des illustrations, non des moyens de preuve; leur fonction est surtout didactique."
15. Leach, *Claude Lévi-Strauss,* 105.
16. *La Pensée sauvage* (Paris: Plon, 1962), 324: "la pensée sauvage est totalisante."
17. *Myth and Meaning* (New York: Shocken, 1979), 40.

18. *The View from Afar*, trans. Joachim Neugroschel and Phoebe Hoss (New York: Basic Books, 1985), 36.

19. *Du Miel aux cendres* (Paris: Plon, 1966), 408: "la puissance et l'inanité de l'événement."

Chapter Two

1. "Réponses," 636.

2. Quoted in Abel, "Sartre vs. Lévi-Strauss," 367.

3. For example, Miriam Glucksmann, *Structuralist Analysis in Contemporary Social Thought* (London: Routledge & Kegan Paul), 78ff.

4. Edward Said, "The Totalitarianism of the Mind," *Kenyon Review* 29, no. 2 (March 1967):256.

5. *L'Homme nu*, 617.

6. *Tristes tropiques* (Paris: Plon, 1955), 39: "L'humanité s'installe dans la monoculture; elle s'apprête à produire la civilisation en masse, comme la betterave."

7. Fredric Jameson, *The Prison-House of Language* (Princeton: Princeton University Press, 1972), 113.

8. *Les Structures élémentaires de la parenté* (Paris: Mouton, 1967), 586: "L'organisation dualiste se réduit à une méthode pour la solution de certains problèmes de la vie sociale."

9. Quoted by Bernard Pingaud, "Comment on devient structuraliste," *L'Arc* (Spring 1967), no. 26, 2: "Le structuralisme refuse tout dualisme. Il est l'union intime du sensible et de l'intellectuel."

10. *Les Structures*, 127, n 19, ff.

11. *Anthropologie structurale* 2 (Paris: Plon, 1973), 161: "La preuve de l'analyse est dans la synthèse: si la synthèse se révèle impossible, c'est que l'analyse est restée incomplète."

12. Michael Riffaterre, "Describing Poetic Structures," in *Structuralism*, ed. Jacques Ehrmann (Garden City: Doubleday, 1970), 196ff.

13. Ricoeur, "Structure et herméneutique," 600 ff.

14. "Le Sorcier et sa magie," *Les Temps modernes*, no. 401 (March 1949):401: "Le problème fondamental est donc celui du rapport entre un individu et le groupe, ou, plus exactement, entre un certain type d'individus et certaines exigences du groupe."

15. *Totemism*, trans. Rodney Needham (Boston: Beacon Press, 1963), 89.

16. *Tristes tropiques*, 54: "Là j'ai commencé à apprendre que tout problème, grave ou futile, peut être liquidé par l'application d'une méthode, toujours identique qui consiste à opposer deux vues traditionnelles de la question."

17. Claude Lévi-Strauss and Roman Jakobson, "Charles Baudelaire's 'Les Chats,' " in Richard and Fernande DeGeorge, ed., *The Structuralists from Marx to Lévi-Strauss* (New York: Anchor, 1972), 127.

18. Lawrence Rosen, "Language, History, and the Logic of Inquiry in Lévi-Strauss and Sartre," *History and Theory* 10, no. 3 (1971):290.
19. Said, "Totalitarianism," 257.

Chapter Three

1. "A Conversation with Claude Lévi-Strauss," *Encounter*, no. 35 (April 1966):35.
2. Paul Ricoeur, "Le Symbolisme et l'explication structurale," *Cahiers internationaux de symbolisme*, no. 4 (1964):91: "le désordre destructeur."
3. *Structural Anthropology*, trans. C. Jakobson and B. G. Schoepf (London: Allen Lane, 1968), 280 ff.
4. "L'Analyse structurale en linguistique et en anthropologie," *Word: Journal of the Linguistic Circle of New York* 1 (1945):47–48: "L'avunculat . . . doit être traité comme une relation intérieure à un systéme . . . qui doit être considéré dans son ensemble pour en apercevoir la structure."
5. Leach, "Anthropologist and Philosopher," 14.
6. Mireille Marc-Lipiansky, *Le Structuralisme de Claude Lévi-Strauss* (Paris: Payot, 1973), 39.
7. *La Pensée sauvage* (Paris: Plon, 1960), 211: "une sorte d'inertie ou d'indifférence logique."
8. *Le Regard éloigné* (Paris: Plon, 1983), 364.
9. "L'Analyse structurale," 50: "le véritable atome de parenté."
10. "Sur les rapports entre la mythologie et le rituel," *Bulletin français de philosophie*, 50, no. 3 (26 May 1956):111.
11. Catherine B. Clément, "La Coupable," in Hélène Cixous, *La Jeune née* (Paris: Union Générale d'Editions, 1975), 58.
12. Ricoeur, "Réponses," 653.
13. Riffaterre, "Describing Poetic Structures," 190.

Chapter Four

1. *Structural Anthropology*, 210. He also described the Oedipus myth (206–18) with all its versions rather than any privileged (for example, that of Sophocles) version.
2. "Avant Propos" in his *L'Identité* (Paris: P.U.F., 1977), 10: "On a raison de dire . . . qu'une traduction n'est jamais parfaite. . . ."
3. "L'Anthropologie devant l'histoire," 637: "Le propre d'un système de signes est d'être transformable, autrement dit, 'traduisible' dans le même langage d'un autre système, à l'aide de permutations."
4. *Tristes tropiques*, 452 ff.
5. "Sur les rapports entre la mythologie et le rituel," 102 ff.
6. *Leçon inaugurale* (Noget le Rotrou: Daupeley-Gouverneur, 1970), 5: "Le propre des mythes . . . n'est-il pas d'évoquer un passé aboli, et

de l'appliquer, comme une grille, sur la dimension du présent, afin d'y
déchiffrer un sens où coincident les deux faces—l'histoire et la structure."

7. *Anthropologie structurale* (Paris: Plon, 1958), 1:234 ff.

8. Glucksmann, *Structuralist Analysis*, 78 ff.

9. "The Structural Study of Myth," *Journal of American Folklore* 78
(October–December 1955), 428 ff.

10. "Réponses," 643: "Je considère parfaitement légitime la recherche par le dedans, par la reprise du sens, sauf que cette reprise, cette
interpretation que les philosophes ou les historiens donneront de leur propre
mythologie. . . ."

11. *Structural Anthropology*, 229.

12. *Dieu existe-t-il?*, ed. Christian Chabanis (Paris: Fayard, 1973),
74.

13. Octavio Paz, *Claude Lévi-Strauss*, trans. J. S. and Maxine Bern-
stein (Ithaca: Cornell University Press, 1970), 39.

14. *L'Homme nu*, 538: "Le propre de tout mythe ou groupe de mythes
est d'interdire qu'on s'y enferme. . . . Le problème se pose et qui, pour
le résoudre, oblige à sortir du cercle que l'analyse s'était tracé."

15. See Armine K. Mortimer, *La Clôture narrative* (Paris: José Corti,
1985) for discussions of the phenomenon of closure inherent in various
narratives throughout time in Western civilization.

16. *L'Origine des manières de table* (Paris: Plon, 1968), 106: "L'histoire
qu'ils [les mythes] racontent n'est pas close."

17. "The Structural Study of Myth," in Richard and Fernande
DeGeorge, ed., *The Structuralists from Marx to Lévi-Strauss* (New York:
Anchor, 1972), 169 ff.

18. "The Story of Asdiwal," in Edmund Leach, ed., *The Structural
Study of Myth and Totemism*, 1–48.

19. Michael Polanyi and Henry Prosch, *Meaning* (Chicago: University
of Chicago Press, 1975), 132.

20. For example, Fredric Jameson, *The Prison-House of Language*, 119:
"Myth is therefore essentially an epistemological, rather than an existential
affair."

21. Cf. Foucault's *Les Mots et les choses* (Paris: Gallimard, 1966) trans.
as *The Order of Things* (New York: Pantheon, 1971).

22. *Le cru et le cuit* (Paris: Plon, 1964), 18: "Si l'esprit humain apparaît
déterminé jusque dans ses mythes, alors 'a fortiori' il doit l'être partout."

23. "Réponses," 643: "[Les mythes] forment le discours de cette
société, et un discours pour lequel il n'y a pas d'émetteur personnel."

24. For example, *Encounter*, 38 ff.

25. *L'homme nu*, 576: "Tout mythe est par nature une traduction, il
a son origine dans un autre mythe provenant d'une population voisine
mais étrangère."

26. "Comment meurent les mythes, *Science et conscience de la société*

1 (1971):132: "On sait, en effet, que les mythes se transforment . . . dans l'espace. [Les transformations] respectent ainsi une sorte de principe de conservation de la matière mythique. . . ."

Chapter Five

1. "Lévi-Strauss en 33 Mots," *Magazine littéraire*, no. 223 (October 1985):27: "Une structure est un système qui demeure identique à travers des transformations."
2. Simone de Beauvoir, Review of *Les Structures élémentaires de la parenté, Les Temps modernes* 5, no. 50 (November 1947):947: "Les cousins croisés sont issus de familles qui se trouvent en position antagoniste, dans un déséquilibre dynamique que seule l'alliance peut résoudre."
3. Jane Gallop, *The Daughter's Seduction* (Ithaca: Cornell University Press, 1982), 133.
4. *The Scope of Anthropology*, trans. Paul and Sherry Paul (London: Jonathan Cape, 1967), 30.
5. Fredric Jameson, *The Prison-House of Language*, 114.
6. Hugo G. Nutini, "Lévi-Strauss' Conception of Science," in *Echanges et communications*, ed. J. Pouillon and P. Maranda (The Hague: Mouton, 1970), 548.
7. T. S. Eliot, *On Poetry and Poets* (London: Faber & Faber, 1957), 112.
8. Riffaterre, "Describing Poetic Structures," 199.
9. *L'Identité*, 10: "[On a raison de dire qu']une traduction n'est jamais parfaite."
10. "L'Anthropologie sociale devant l'histoire," *Annales: economies, sociétés, civilisations* 15, no. 4 (1960):629: " 'Qu'est-ce que tout cela signifie?' Et, pour y répondre, nous nous efforçons de 'traduire', dans nôtre langage, des règles primitivement données dans un langage différent."
11. Ibid.: "Le propre d'un système de signes est d'être transformable, autrement dit 'traduisible' dans le langage d'un autre système, à l'aide de permutations."
12. *La Voie des masques*, 144: "Comme un mythe, un masque nie autant qu'il affirme; il n'est pas fait seulement de ce qu'il dit ou croit dire, mais de ce qu'il exclut."
13. "Réponses," 634: "Le système des postulats et des axiomes requis pour fonder un code, permettant de traduire avec le moins mauvais rendement possible, 'l'autre' dans 'le nôtre' et réciproquement. . . ."
14. "Discussion," in his *L'Identité*, 42: "Il s'agit toujours de savoir si une certaine combinatoire n'est pas susceptible d'expression spatiale."
15. Raymond Bellour and Catherine Clément, "Claude Lévi-Strauss," in their *Structuralisme et écologie* (Paris: Gallimard, 1979), 474: "Ces transformations réciproques s'engendrent par symétrie et inversion, de sorte que les mythes se réfléchissent mutuellement selon tel ou tel axe."

16. "Réponses à quelques questions," 652: "L'homme de science que j'essaie d'être."

17. Robert M. Pirsig, *Zen and the Art of Motorcycle Maintenance* (New York: William Morrow, 1984), 59 ff.

18. "L'Anthropologie sociale devant l'histoire," 629: "Le signe étant, selon la célèbre définition de Peirce, 'ce qui remplace quelque chose pour quelqu'un'. . . . ."

19. Heusch, "Anthropologie structurale," 54: "En fait, ce sont des codes différents, transmettant le même message."

20. *La Potière jalouse* (Paris: Plon, 1985), 268: "Signifier n'est jamais qu'établir une relation entre les termes."

21. Georges Charbonnier, ed., *Entretiens avec Claude Lévi-Strauss* (Paris: 10/18, 1961), 46 ff.

22. Bellour and Clément, "Claude Lévi-Strauss," 474: "les mythes sont toujours réductibles aux autres au moyen de transformations de ce type [les mythes des tribus nord-américaines]."

23. "La Notion de structure en ethnologie," *Janua linguarum* 16 (1962):43: "Il faut . . . poser le primat du changement, et considérer la structure comme la manière dont se traduit, pour l'observateur, une appréhension instantanée et artificielle d'une réalité mouvementée."

24. *Structural Anthropology*, 229.

25. Greimas, *Du Sens,* 113: "C'est une meilleure connaissance des modèles de transformation dont ils [les historiens] ont également besoin."

Chapter Six

1. *Totemism,* 99.

2. *Les Structures élémentaires de la parenté,* 6: "C'est, en apparence, l'opposition entre le comportement humain et le comportement animal, qui fournit la plus frappante illustration de l'antinomie de la culture et de la nature."

3. *Tristes tropiques,* 59: "L'ethnographie est une des rares vocations authentiques: on peut la découvrir en soi, même sans qu'on vous l'ait enseignée."

4. *Les Structures,* 28.

5. *Totemism,* 65.

6. "Le Triangle culinaire," *L'Arc,* no. 26 (1965):21: "[La culture est] une médiation des rapports de l'homme et du monde."

7. *Les Structures,* 9 ff.

8. *Le Cru et le cuit,* 20: "[Nous prétendons montrer comment] les mythes se pensent dans les hommes et à leur insu."

9. Yvan Simonis, *Claude Lévi-Strauss ou la passion de l'inceste* (Paris: Aubier-Montaigne, 1968), 35: "Distinguer nature et culture est utile en bonne méthode logique, mais il est difficile, et même impossible, de retrouver une distinction aussi nette dans l'homme existant concret."

10. "The Family," in *Man, Culture and Society,* ed. Harry L. Shapiro (New York: Oxford University Press, 1960), 277–78.

11. *L'Origine des manières de table,* 153.

12. "History and Dialectic," in Richard and Fernande DeGeorge, ed., *The Structuralists from Marx to Lévi-Strauss,* 209.

13. Leach, *Claude Lévi-Strauss,* 11 ff.

14. "History and Dialectic," 211 n. 1.

15. *Le Cru et le cuit,* 152: "Les Ge font de l'ensemble (cru + pourri) une catégorie naturelle; les Tupi font de l'ensemble (cru + pourri) une catégorie culturelle."

16. Martin Heidegger, *On the Way to Language,* trans. Peter D. Hertz (New York: Harper & Row, 1971), 21.

17. "The Structural Study of Myth," 179.

18. Hayden White, *Tropics of Discourse* (Baltimore: Johns Hopkins University Press, 1978), 183–96.

19. *Les Structures élémentaires de la parenté,* 561.

20. *Du Miel aux cendres,* 201: "La mythologie de la cuisine se déroule dans le bon sens . . . celui du passage de la nature à la culture, tandis que la mythologie du miel procède à contre-courant, en regressant de la culture à la nature."

21. *La Pensée sauvage,* 170: "L'échange matrimonial opère donc à la façon d'un mécanisme médiateur entre une nature et une culture posées d'abord comme disjointes."

22. "The Family," in *Man, Culture, and Society,* ed. Harry L. Shapiro, 346.

23. *Totemism,* 65 ff.

24. "History and Dialectic," 211 ff.

Chapter Seven

1. "L'Anthropologie sociale devant l'histoire," 44: "les sociétés n'ont pas d'histoire."

2. *Race et histoire* (Paris: Gonthier, 1961), 38: "Le 'Progrès' n'est ni nécessaire, ni continu: il procède par sauts et par bonds, ou comme diraient les biologistes, par mutations."

3. Charbonnier, *Entretiens,* 71: "L'Histoire était une catégorie intérieure à certaines sociétés, un mode selon lequel les sociétés hiérarchisées s'appréhendent elles-mêmes et non pas un milieu . . . [pour] tous les groupes humaines."

4. See his discussion of the distinctiveness of social anthropology from Western history in his 1960 acceptance lecture at the Collège de France in his *Leçon inaugurale,* 21 ff.

5. *The Scope of Anthropology,* 49.

6. *La Pensée sauvage,* 347: "L'Histoire n'est qu'une méthode, à la-

quelle ne correspond pas un objet distinct"; 336: "Dans le système de Sartre, l'Histoire joue très précisément le rôle d'un mythe."

7. Abel, "Sartre vs. Lévi-Strauss," 367 ff.

8. *La Pensée sauvage*, 339: "L'ethnologue respecte l'histoire, mais il ne lui accorde pas une valeur privilégiée."

9. "Comment meurent les mythes," in his *Science et conscience de la société* (Paris: Calmann-Levy, 1971), 143; "un svant et un philosophe qui n'a jamais consenti à faire de l'Histoire un lieu privilégié où l'homme serait assuré de pouvoir trouver sa vérité."

10. Cf. George Steiner, in *Encounter*, 33: "our theory of history and of cultural hierarchy is profoundly 'un-Marxian.' " Also Henri Lefebvre, "Claude Lévi-Strauss et le nouvel eléatisme," *L'Homme et la société* 1 (1967):29 ff.

11. *Anthropologie structurale* 1:17: "Seul le développement historique permet de soupeser et d'évaluer dans leurs valeurs respectifs les éléments du présent."

12. Leach, *Claude Lévi-Strauss*, 9.

13. "Sur les rapports entre la mythologie et le rituel," 124: "condamné à l'étude statique: l'Histoire est ce qui lui manque le plus."

14. Cited in Abel, "Sartre vs. Lévi-Strauss," 367.

15. Cited in Sanche de Gramont, "There are no superior societies," in E. Nelson and Tanya Hayes, ed., *Claude Lévi-Strauss: The Anthropologist as Hero* (Cambridge: MIT Press, 1970), 21.

16. "Le Rôle du Philosophe," *Magazine littéraire*, no. 225 (December 1985):59: "tout ce qui était vraiment créateur, tout ce qui bouleversait nos idées sur l'homme et nos façons de penser, venait de la science."

17. "Le Temps du mythe," *Annales: economies, sociétés, civilisations*, no. 3 (1971):537: ". . . l'ordre rêvé depuis toujours par les mythes eux-mêmes."

18. "L'Anthropologie sociale devant l'histoire," 633: "Les sociétés existantes sont le résultat des grandes transformations survenues dans l'esprit humain; . . . une chaîne ininterrompue d'événements réels relie ces faits à ceux que nous pouvons observer."

19. *Anthropologie structurale*, 2:325: "C'est donc l'Histoire, conjugée avec la sociologie et la sémeiologie, qui doit permettre à l'analyste de briser le cercle d'une confrontation intemporelle."

20. *Leçon*, 23: "Certains faits relèvent d'un temps statique et irreversible, d'autres, d'un temps mécanique et réversible. . . ."

21. *Du miel aux cendres*, 408: "L'analyse structurale ne récuse donc pas l'histoire . . . et lui concède une place de premier plan . . . par s'incliner devant la puissance et l'inanité de l'événement."

22. Ricoeur, "Le Symbolisme et l'explication structurale," 95 ff.

23. "La Notion de structure en ethnologie," *Janua Linguarum* 16 (1962):45: "Sans oublier qu'un historien peut parfois travailler en eth-

nologue et un ethnologue en historien, . . . même les sciences de l'homme
ont leurs relations d'incertitude."
    24. E.g., *Anthropologie structurale,* 1:31.
    25. *Tristes tropiques,* 58.

Chapter Eight
    1. *Tristes tropiques,* 224.
    2. *La Voie des masques,* 19: ". . . pour objet d'expliquer leur origine
légendaire ou surnaturel et de fonder leur [les mythes] rôle dans le
rituel, l'économie, la société. . . ."
    3. Ibid., 29.
    4. Ibid., 27.
    5. Ibid., 102.
    6. *Anthropologie structurale,* 1:62.
    7. *La Pensée sauvage,* 294: ". . . une observation attentive et mé-
ticuleuse tout entière tournée vers le concret, trouve dans le symbolisme,
à la fois son principe et son aboutissement."
    8. "Réponses," 632: "Le sens n'est pas directement perçu mais
déduit."
    9. *Du miel aux cendres,* 74 ff.
    10. *Le Regard éloigné,* 201 ff.
    11. Ricoeur, "Le Symbolisme," 96: "Un symbole ne symbolise que
dans une structure à un moment donné mais cette structure représente
une coupe de rationalité à un moment donné. . . ."
    12. *Le Regard éloigné,* 201: "une nette symétrie . . . ils répondent
à des exigences mentales du même type, tournées soit vers le corps, soit
vers la société et le monde."
    13. Richard A. Shweder, "A Slash-and-Burn Intellect," *New York
Times Book Review,* 13 April 1985, p. 39.
    14. "Le Sorcier et sa magie," *Les Temps modernes* 4, no. 41 (March
1949):404: "La cure met en relation ces rôles opposés, assure le passage
l'un à l'autre et manifeste, dans une expérience totale, les cohérences de
l'univers psychique, la même projection de l'univers social."
    15. *Totemism,* 78.
    16. *A World on the Wane,* trans. John Russell (London: Hutchinson,
1961), 160.
    17. *Anthropologie structurale,* 1:71: ". . . assez profondément pour
. . . élaborer une sorte de code universel, capable d'exprimer les propriétés
communes aux structures spécifiques."
    18. "Réponses," 632.
    19. *La Pensée sauvage,* 143: "Si, par le moyen des prohibitions ali-
mentaires, les hommes dénient une nature animale réelle à leur humanité,
c'est parce qu'il leur faut assumer les caractères symboliques . . . pour
créer des différences. . . ."

20. *Le Regard éloigné*, 146: "Les contraintes propres au fonctionne-ment de la pensée . . . orientent la formation des symboles . . . [et] expliquent comment ils s'opposent et s'articulent entre eux."

21. *Les Structures élémentaires de la parenté*, 568: "L'émergence de la pensée symbolique devait exiger que les femmes, comme les paroles, fussent des choses qui s'échangent."

22. *L'Origine des manières de table*, 68: "Le vocabulaire qu'ils [les mythes] utilisent renvoie à trois ordres séparés."

Chapter Nine

1. Leach, "Anthropologist and Philosopher," 20.

2. *Le Cru et le cuit*, 20: ". . . comment les mythes se pensent sans les hommes et à leur insu."

3. *Anthropologie structurale*, 1:91: "Révéler les secrets ressorts qui . . . mouvent l'esprit humain."

4. Ibid., 254: "La répétition a une fonction propre, qui est de rendre manifeste la structure du mythe."

5. Charbonnier, *Entretiens*, 83 ff.

6. "Réponses," 648: "L'esprit humain . . . ce qui m'intéresse c'est de savoir comment il fonctionne."

7. Jean-François Lyotard, "Les Indiens ne cueillent pas les fleurs," *Annales: économies, sociétés, civilisations* 20, no. 1 (January 1965):69: "La pensée sauvage n'est pas un je pense, mais un ça pense: ce penser est entendre et correspondre."

8. *Le Regard éloigné*, 60: "La masse des règles inconscientes demeure la plus importante et reste la plus efficace [de notre patrimonie biolo-gique]."

9. In *Dieu existe-t-il?*, 76: ". . . nous sommes assis sur quelque chose ou adossé à quelque chose que nous ne voyons pas parce que nous avons le dos contre."

10. *Anthropologie structurale*, 1:31 ff.

11. Charbonnier, *Entretiens*, 83: "Les sociétés dites primitives recon-naissent avec plus d'objectivité le rôle de l'activité inconsciente dans la création esthétique et manipule avec une étonnante clairvoyance cette vie obscure de l'esprit."

12. "L'Anthropologie sociale devant l'histoire," 635: "L'infra-sys-tème inconsciente est dynamique et déséquilibrée, fait, à la fois, du legs du passé et de tendances d'avenir, non encore réalisées."

13. *Totemism*, 104.

14. *Anthropologie structurale*, 1:224: "L'inconscient est toujours vide . . . il se borne à imposer des lois structurales, qui épuisent sa réalité, à des éléments inarticulés qui proviennent d'ailleurs."

15. Ricoeur, "Le Symbolisme et l'explication structurale," 85.

16. Ricoeur, "Structure et herméneutique," 600.

17. Ricoeur, "Le Symbolisme," 85.

18. Said, "Totalitarianism," 259.

Chapter Ten

1. "L'Anthropologie sociale devant l'histoire," 637.

2. *The Scope of Anthropology*, 52.

3. "Panorama de l'ethnologie," 121: "L'ethnologie . . . consiste dans l'aspect scientifique de toutes les recherches concernant l'homme."

4. de Gramont, "There are no superior societies," 7.

5. *Tristes tropiques*, 452: "A cet âge du mythe, sa seule humanité faisait de lui un esclave."

6. Robert Goedecke, "Lévi-Strauss out of his langue," *Philosophy Today* 22 (Spring 1978):82.

7. *La Pensée sauvage*, 165: "Les castes posent les femmes comme hétérogènes naturellement, les groupes totémiques les posent comme hétérogènes culturellement."

8. *L'Origine des manières de table*, 421: "Si les femmes surtout ont besoin d'éducation, c'est qu'elles sont des êtres périodiques."

9. *Du Miel aux cendres*, 252: "La femme, éternellement sarigue et renarde, est incapable de surmonter sa nature contradictoire et d'atteindre à une perfection."

10. Gallop, *The Daughter's Seduction*, 133.

11. Georges Bataille, *L'Erotisme* (Paris: Minuit, 1957), 231.

12. "The Family," in Harry L. Shapiro, ed., *Man, Culture, Society* (London: Oxford University Press, 1971), 356.

13. Raymond Aron, "Le Paradoxe du même et de l'autre," in J. Pouillon and P. Mara, ed., *Echanges et communications* (The Hague: Mouton, 1970), 944.

14. *Race et histoire*, 24: "L'humanité devient une et identique à elle-même; seulement, cette unité et cette identité ne peuvent se réaliser que progressivement et la variété des cultures illustre les moments d'un processus. . . ."

15. *Les Structures elémentaires de la parenté*, 569: "Elle [la femme] est tout de même une personne, et . . . dans la mesure où on la définit comme signe, on s'oblige à reconnaître en elle un producteur de signes."

16. *Totemism*, 53–54.

17. *Tristes tropiques*, 39: "L'humanité s'installe dans la monoculture; elle s'apprête à produire la civilisation en masse, comme la betterave."

18. Robert Goedecke, "Lévi-Strauss out of his langue," 80.

19. Cited in de Gramont, "There are no superior societies," 10.

20. "Sur les rapports entre la mythologie et le rituel," 122: ". . . nous ne pouvons pas rester enfermés au sein d'une société."

21. *Le Regard éloigné*, 80.

22. Cited by Cathérine Clément, "La Bonne distance," *Magazine littéraire*, no. 197 (July 1983):66: "La race . . . est une fonction parmi d'autres de la culture."

23. *Race et histoire*, 85: "une attitude dynamique qui consiste à prévoir, à comprendre et prémouvoir ce qui veut être."

24. Cathérine Backès-Clément, *Lévi-Strauss ou la structure du malheur* (Paris: Seghers, 1974), 186: "Lévi-Strauss est parti pour situer l'ethnologie comme gardienne d'un certain humanisme."

25. "Panorama de l'ethnologie (1950–1957)," 120 ff.

26. "Réponses à quelques questions," 633: "Je n'ai pas voulu faire une philosophie; j'ai simplement essayé de me rendre compte, pour mon profit personnel, des implications philosophiques de certains aspects de mon travail."

27. *L'Origine des manières de table*, 422.

28. Derrida, *Nature, culture, écriture*, 49: "La seule faiblesse du bricolage . . . c'est de ne pouvoir se justifier de part en part en son propre discours."

29. Simonis, *Claude Lévi-Strauss ou la passion*, 131: ". . . il devient inepte à le [l'humanisme] penser positivement."

30. Neville Dyson-Hudson, "Structure and Infra-Structure in Primitive Society," in *The Structuralist Controversy* (Baltimore: Johns Hopkins University Press, 1972), 225.

31. *Race et histoire*, 17: "Beaucoup de coutumes sont nées . . . de la seule volonté de ne pas demeurer en reste par rapport à un groupe voisin qui soumettait à un usage précis un domaine où l'on n'avait pas songé à . . . règles."

32. Cf. Mireille Marc-Lipiansky, *Le Structuralisme de Lévi-Strauss* (Paris: Payot, 1973), 240 ff.

33. Gaston Bachelard, *Le Nouvel Esprit scientifique* (Paris: PUF, 1983), 6: "Tôt ou tard, c'est la pensée philosophique qui deviendra le thème fondamental de la polémique philosophique: cette pensée conduira à substituer aux métaphysiques intuitives et immédiates les métaphysiques discursives objectivement rectifiées."

34. "Les Mathématiques de l'homme," *Esprit* 24, no. 10 (1956):525: "C'est vers l'homme, bien plus que vers le monde physique, que s'orientent les spéculations des premiers géomètres et arithméticiens."

35. *Encounter*, 33.

36. "Panorama de l'ethnologie," 121: "l'ethnologie consiste dans l'aspect scientifique de toutes les recherches concernant l'homme."

37. Greimas, *Du Sens*, 32–33.

38. *Le Regard éloigné*, 48: "Des échanges trop faciles égalisent et confondent leur [la race humaine] diversité."

39. "L'Anthropologie sociale devant l'histoire," 631: "Les hommes

communiquent au moyen de symboles et de signes; pour l'anthropologie, qui est une conversation de l'homme avec l'homme, tout est symbole et signe, qui se pose comme intermédiaire entre deux objets."

40. *La Pensée sauvage,* 326: "Nous croyons que le dernier but des sciences humaines n'est pas de constituer l'homme, mais de le dissoudre."

41. Honoré de Balzac, *Louis Lambert,* in *La Comédie humaine,* X (Paris: Pléiade, 1950):10:396: "Les idées sont en nous un système complet, semblable à l'un des règnes de la nature, une sorte de floraison dont l'iconographie sera retracée par un homme de génie qui passera pour fou peut-être."

Selected Bibliography

PRIMARY SOURCES

(Note: French books are published in Paris by Plon unless otherwise stated.)

Anthropologie structurale, vol. 1. 1958. Translated by Claire Jacobson and Brooke G. Schoepfe as *Structural Anthropology.* New York: Basic Books, 1963; London: Penguin, 1968.

Anthropologie structurale, vol. 2. 1973. Translated by Monique Layton as *Structural Anthropology,* vol. 2. Chicago: University of Chicago Press, 1976.

"Charles Baudelaire's 'Les Chats.' " *L'Homme* 2 (January–April 1962):5–21. Translated by F.M. DeGeorge in *The Structuralists from Marx to Lévi-Strauss,* ed. Richard and Fernande DeGeorge. New York: Anchor, 1972. (Roman Jakobson was co-author.)

Entretiens avec Claude Lévi-Strauss. Edited by Georges Charbonnier. Paris: Plon-Juillard, 1961. Translated by John and Doreen Weightman as *Conversations with Claude Lévi-Strauss.* London: Jonathan Cape, 1969.

Leçon inaugurale. Noget le Rotrou: Daupeley Gouverneur, 1970. Translated by Sherry O. Paul and Robert A. Paul as *The Scope of Anthropology.* London: Jonathan Cape, 1967. (This lecture was given on the occasion of his appointment to the Collège de France in 1960.)

Myth and Meaning. Toronto: Toronto University Press, 1978; New York: Shocken, 1979. (Talks in English from CBC Radio series "Ideas," December 1977).

Mythologiques, 1. Le Cru et le cuit. 1964. Translated by John and Doreen Weightman as *The Raw and the Cooked.* New York: Harper & Row, 1969.

Mythologiques, 2. Du Miel aux cendres. 1966. Translated by John and Doreen Weightman as *From Honey to Ashes.* Chicago: University of Chicago Press, 1973.

Mythologiques, 3. L'Origine des manières de table. 1968. Translated by John and doreen Weightman as *The Origin of Table Manners.* New York: Harper & Row, 1978.

Mythologiques, 4. L'Homme nu. 1971. Translated by John and Doreen Weightman as *The Naked Man.* New York: Harper & Row, 1981.

Paroles données. 1984. Translated by Roy Willis as *Anthropology and Myth.* Oxford and New York; Blackwell, 1986.

116

La Pensée sauvage. 1962. Translated as *The Savage Mind.* Chicago: University of Chicago Press, 1966; London: Wedenfeld & Nicolson, 1966.

La Potière jalouse. 1985.

Race et histoire. New York: UNESCO, 1952. Translated as *Race and History.* New York: UNESCO, 1952.

Le Regard éloigné. 1983. Translated by Joachim Neugroschel and Pheobe Hoss as *The View from Afar.* London: Blackwell, 1985.

Les Structures élémentaires de la parenté. Paris: Presses Universitaires de France, 1949. 2d ed. The Hague: Mouton, 1967. Translated by James Harle Bell and John R. von Sturner as *The Elementary Structures of Kinship.* Boston: Beacon Press, 1969.

Le Totémisme aujourd'hui. Paris, Presses Universitaires de France, 1962. Translated by Rodney Needham as *Totemism.* Boston: Beacon Press, 1963; London, Merlin Press, 1964.

Tristes Tropiques. 1955. Rev. ed. 1968. Translated by John Russell as *A World on the Wane.* London: Hutchinson & Company, 1961. Chapters 14, 15, 16, and 39 omitted. Also translated as *Tristes Tropiques.* New York: Atheneum, 1963.

La Vie familiale et sociale des Indiens Nambikwara. Paris: Société des Américanistes, 1948.

La Voie des masques. Geneva: Ed. d'Art d'Albert Skira, 1975. 2d ed.: Plon, 1979. Translated by Sylvia Modelski as *The Way of the Masks.* Seattle: University of Washington Press, 1982.

For comprehensive bibliographies of his articles, see:

1) Hayes, Eugene and Tanya, eds. *Claude Lévi-Strauss: The Anthropologist as Hero.* Cambridge: MIT Press, 1970.

2) Pace, David. *Claude Lévi-Strauss: The Bearer of Ashes.* Boston: Routledge & Kegan Paul, 1983.

3) Simonis, Yves. *Claude Lévi-Strauss ou la passion de l'inceste.* Paris: Aubier-Montaigne, 1968.

SECONDARY SOURCES

1. Books

Badiou, A. *Le Concept de Modèle.* Paris: Maspero, 1969. Lévi-Strauss used a philosophical and ideological model rather than a scientific one.

Glucksmann, Miriam. *Structural Analysis in Contemporary Social Thought.* London: Routledge & Kegan Paul, 1974. Ph.D. thesis, University of London. Thorough review of predecessors to Lévi-Strauss.

Hayes, Eugene and Tanya, eds. *Claude Lévi-Strauss: The Anthropologist as Hero.* Cambridge: MIT Press, 1970. Essays by Leach, Stuart Hughes, Steiner, Caws, et al.

Lapointe, François and Claire. *Claude Lévi-Strauss and His Critics.* New York: Garland, 1977. Critical review of primary and secondary bibliographical listings.

Leach, Edmund. *Claude Lévi-Strauss.* New York: Viking Press, 1970. A social anthropologist skeptically reviews the Lévi-Strauss opus.

Marc-Lipiansky, Mireille. *Le Structuralisme de Lévi-Strauss.* Paris: Payot, 1973. Lévi-Strauss is a philosopher despite his intentions to be a scientist. His method will survive because of its rigor and fecundity. Validity of the philosophy of structuralism is contested.

Milet, Albert. *Pour ou contre le structuralisme.* Tournon: Ed. C.D.C., 1968. Overview of life and works until 1966.

Sartre, Jean-Paul. *Critique de la raison dialectique.* Paris: Gallimard 1960, 104 ff. Takes Lévi-Strauss to task for not being a dialectical thinker.

Simonis, Yves. *Claude Lévi-Strauss ou la passion de l'inceste.* Paris: Aubier-Montaigne, 1968. Good introduction but limited by publication date.

2. Articles and Reviews

Alverson, Hoyt. "Phonology and the Foundations of Lévi-Strauss' Structuralism." *American Journal of Semiotics* 2, no. 4 (1984):99–123. Rebuttal of phonemic taxonomy as a viable model for cultural functioning.

Barthes, Roland. "Pour une psycho-sociology de l'alimentation." *Annales,* no. 5 (September–October 1961):977–86. Adaptation of Lévi-Strauss's "gustèmes" to a philosophical mode.

Beauvoir, Simone de. Review of *Les Structures elémentaires de la parenté. Les Temps modernes* 50, 1, no. 50 (November 1949):943 ff. Salient features of Lévi-Strauss study.

Gardner, Howard. "Structural Analysis." *Semiotica,* 5, no. 1 (1972):31–57. Helpful distinctions between Piaget and Lévi-Strauss in their views of structuralism.

Heusch, Luc de. "Anthropologie structurale et symbolique." *Cahiers internationaux de symbolisme* 2 (1963):51–65. Insightful comparisons between Gaston Bachelard's symbols and *La Pensée Sauvage* by Lévi-Strauss regarding their scientific methods.

Pouillon, Jean. "Sartre et Lévi-Strauss." *L'Arc,* no. 26 (1967):60–65. Contrast between Sartre's "praxis" and Lévi-Strauss's "structure."

Ricoeur, Paul. "Le symbolisme et l'explication structurale." *Cahiers internationaux de symbolisme,* no. 4 (1964):81–96. Shows deficiencies of structuralist method by reference to assumptions of hermeneutics.

Ricoeur, Paul. "Structure et herméneutique." *Esprit,* 31 (November 1963):600 ff. Develops notion of "Kantian unconscious" in works by Lévi-Strauss.

Riffaterre, Michael. "Describing Poetic Structures." In *Structuralism,* ed. Jacques Ehrmann, 196 ff. Garden City: Doubleday, 1970. Rejection of scientific pretensions of structuralism as valid literary criticism based on Lévi-Strauss's exposition of Baudelaire's "Les Chats."

Rosen, Lawrence. "Language, History, and the Logic of Inquiry in Lévi-Strauss and Sartre," *History and Theory*, 10, no. 3 (1971):290 ff. Stakes in debate between Sartre and Lévi-Strauss.

3. Bibliographies:

Harari, Josue, ed. *Structuralists and Structuralisms*. Ithaca: Diacritics, 1971. Pp. 37 ff.

Layton, Monique. In her trans. of Claude Lévi-Strauss, *Structural Anthropology*, 2. Chicago: University of Chicago Press, 1976. Pp. 363–72.

Miller, Joan M. *French Structuralism*. New York: Garland, 1981. Pp. 306–34.

Index

Oedipus myth, 38, 39, 56, 105
onion, 83, 102
order, 16, 22, 26, 30, 31, 37, 53–54,
    62, 65
organicism, 15, 18, 37, 44, 52, 55,
    57, 62, 65, 93, 95, 96
outside, 1, 2, 3, 23, 46, 77, 87, 98,
    102

paradigm, 39, 40
Paz, Octavio, 25, 37, 106
Peirce, Charles, 45, 48, 108
phenomenology, 55, 90
philosophy, 2, 3, 11, 19, 28, 53, 86–
    87, 93, 94, 95, 103, 114
phonology, 4, 12
Pingaud, Bernard, 26, 104
Pirsig, Robert, 47, 108
poetics, 3, 10, 14, 21, 54, 57, 59–60,
    89
Polanyi, Michael, 39, 106
polarities, 9, 13, 25, 28, 54, 64, 70,
    98
Prague School, 4, 14, 48, 80
primitive mind, 46, 49, 53, 80, 91
Pritchard, Evans, 92
progress, 2, 10, 14, 21, 54, 57, 59–
    60, 89
Propp, Vladimir, 21, 27, 29
psychoanalysis, 2, 46, 47, 62, 79
psycholinguistics, 77

racism, 14, 25, 58, 88–89, 92, 94,
    98, 102
Radcliffe-Brown, Alfred, 11
real, 76, 77–85
referent, 48, 77
repertory of ideas, 73, 74
Ricoeur, Paul, 7, 27, 30, 32, 38, 64,
    65, 71, 72, 84, 92, 93, 103, 105,
    114
Riffaterre, Michael, 4, 7, 27, 32, 44,
    71, 104, 105, 107
rituals, 11, 14, 15, 20, 21, 22, 36, 79
Roman, Monique, 6
Rosen, Lawrence, 28, 105

Rousseau, Jean-Jacques, 2, 10, 11, 21,
    35, 38, 47, 51, 53, 57, 87, 91, 94,
    96, 105, 110, 111, 112, 113
rules, 31, 45, 80, 86, 88, 96, 107
Russell, John, 7

Said, Edward, 24, 28, 85, 104, 105
Sartre, Jean-Paul, 6–7, 19, 26, 27, 54,
    55, 71, 92–93
Saussure, Ferdinand de, 48, 80
savage mind, 14, 15, 54, 55, 91
schematics, 8, 17, 31, 32, 37, 39, 43,
    70
science, 4, 95; scientific method, 15,
    19, 20, 23, 27, 65, 72, 84–85, 86–
    87, 94; Lévi-Strauss as scientist, 6,
    29, 47, 72, 90
semiotics, 36, 41, 48, 49, 52, 64, 67,
    70, 86, 95, 96–97, 98, 102
series musical, 17
Serres, Michel, 19
shamans, 72
Shweder, Richard, 72, 111
signified, 48, 77, 78
signifier, 48, 77
Simonis, Yvan, 53, 93, 108, 114
social anthropology, 6, 11, 20, 21, 22,
    36, 45, 60, 86, 94
social sciences, 15, 20, 21, 43, 92; and
    linguistics, 4, 12
sociobiology, 16
sociology, 2, 11, 12, 18, 20, 40, 52,
    64
Sorbonne, 2, 6, 23, 71, 84, 86, 94
stationary society, 14
Steiner, Georges, 61, 110
story, 27, 28, 29, 32, 55, 59–60, 87
storytelling, 5, 8, 17, 25, 27, 30, 31,
    33, 35, 38, 54, 55, 56, 63, 69, 70,
    81
structuralism, 6, 7, 19, 22, 26, 42,
    43, 60, 64, 93; vs. formalism, 6,
    21; historical, 64; method, 7, 13,
    19, 20, 26; structuralist, 28, 40, 41,
    44, 59, 61, 62, 81
structure, 12, 16, 20, 21, 28, 29–33,
    41, 50, 70, 72, 80, 83, 86, 92, 94